McClelland and Stewart
The Canadian Publishers
481 University Avenue
Toronto M5G 2E9

Canadian Cataloguing in Publication Data

Aislin.
Old whores

ISBN 0-7710-6521-3

1. Canada – Politics and government – 1984-1987 – Caricatures and cartoons.* 2. World politics – 1985-1987 – Caricatures and cartoons. 3. Canadian wit and humor, Pictorial. I. Title.

NC1449.A47A4 1987 971.064'7'0207 C87-094229-8

Other Books by Aislin
Aislin – 100 Caricatures (1971)
Hockey Night in Moscow (1972, with Jack Ludwig)
Aislin – 150 Caricatures (1973)
The Great Hockey Thaw (1974, with Jack Ludwig)
'Ello, Morgentaler? Aislin – 150 Caricatures (1975)
O.K. Everybody Take a Valium! Aislin – 150 Caricatures (1977)
l'Humour d'Aislin (1977)
The Retarded Giant (1977, with Bill Mann)
The Hecklers: A History of Canadian Political Cartooning (1979, with Peter Desbarats)
The Year the Expos Almost Won the Pennant! (1979, with Brodie Snyder)
Did the Earth Move? Aislin – 180 Caricatures (1980)
The Year the Expos Finally Won Something (1981, with Brodie Snyder)
The First Great Canadian Sports Trivia Quiz Book (1981, with Brodie Snyder)
Stretchmarks (1982)
The Anglo Guide to Survival in Quebec (1983, with various Montreal writers)
Tootle: A Children's Story (1984, with John Sarrazin)
Where's the Trough? (1985)

Printed and bound in Canada

Special thanks to Peter Arsenault for helping me put this material together; to Charis Wahl, my editor, for getting it right; and to John Knowles, just for being there. – T.M.

OLD WHORES

More AISLIN cartoons

M&S

INTRODUCTION

蘿蔔雲吞

把蘿蔔刨碎。

把調味料加入肉末中，拌勻，然後再加入蘿蔔混合。

葱切碎；青菜切 5 厘米度；煎蛋切細。

用碗裝醬油、麻油、胡椒及味精，放入葱及蛋。

用雲吞皮包餡料②，放在開水中煮熟，加入青菜同滾。

把⑤倒入④中，拌勻即成。

CHARLIE MACKENZIE
PRESIDENT-FOR-LIFE
RHINOCEROS PARTY.

THIS COLLECTION IS
DEDICATED TO M.T.,
THE GAZOO'S
QUEEN BEE.

⇨ THE TORIES - PART ONE...

SO, RICHARD, WHAT WILL WE DO WITH TONS OF RANCID TUNA?
SMOKE IT? SNORT IT?
AISLIN 85.
MONTREAL GAZETTE

·OUTCRY OVER PROPOSED PENSION CHANGES.

·WESTERN BANKS FOLD.

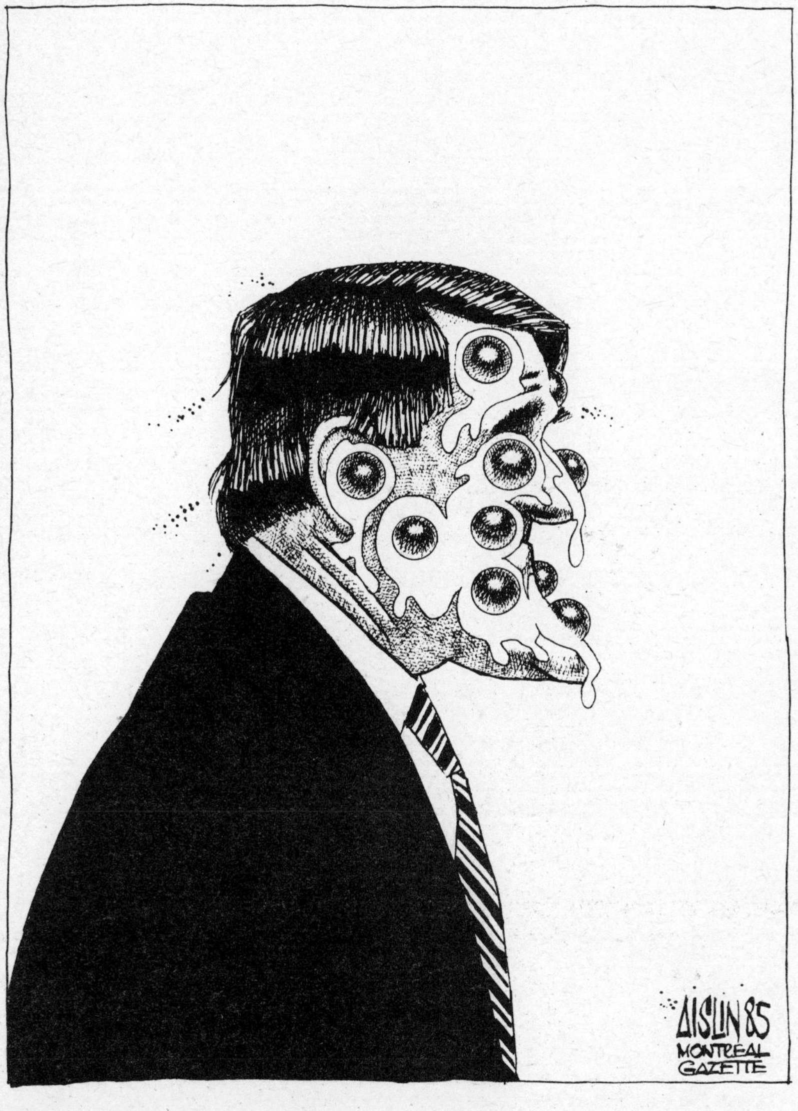

• BLACK SEPTEMBER.

LIKE WITH THE TUNA, EH?
WE WENT BOOMP...AH..
BUMP-BUMP-BOING!!!
UMM...TAKE THAT JOHN FRASER!
...RUT-A-TUT-TUT-TILT...
BANG!
AISLIN 86.
MONTREAL GAZETTE
• IN N.Y. TIMES INTERVIEW, P.M. EXAGGERATES HIS "EXPEDITIOUS" HANDLING OF THE TUNA SCANDAL.

THE IDEAL SPEAKER...
·JOHN FRASER OF TUNA FAME APPOINTED HOUSE SPEAKER.
...CONSIDERING THE UNLIKELY POSSIBILITY OF ANY SALADE NIÇOISE OR TUNA CASSEROLE JOKES...
AISLIN 86
MONTREAL GAZETTE

·FEDS "FORGET" TO TELL NEWFOUNDLAND ABOUT NEW FISHING ARRANGEMENT WITH FRANCE.

AISLIN 87. MONTREAL GAZETTE

NEWS ITEM: BLAIS-GRENIER FINALLY QUITS CABINET...
AISLIN 86
MONTREAL GAZETTE

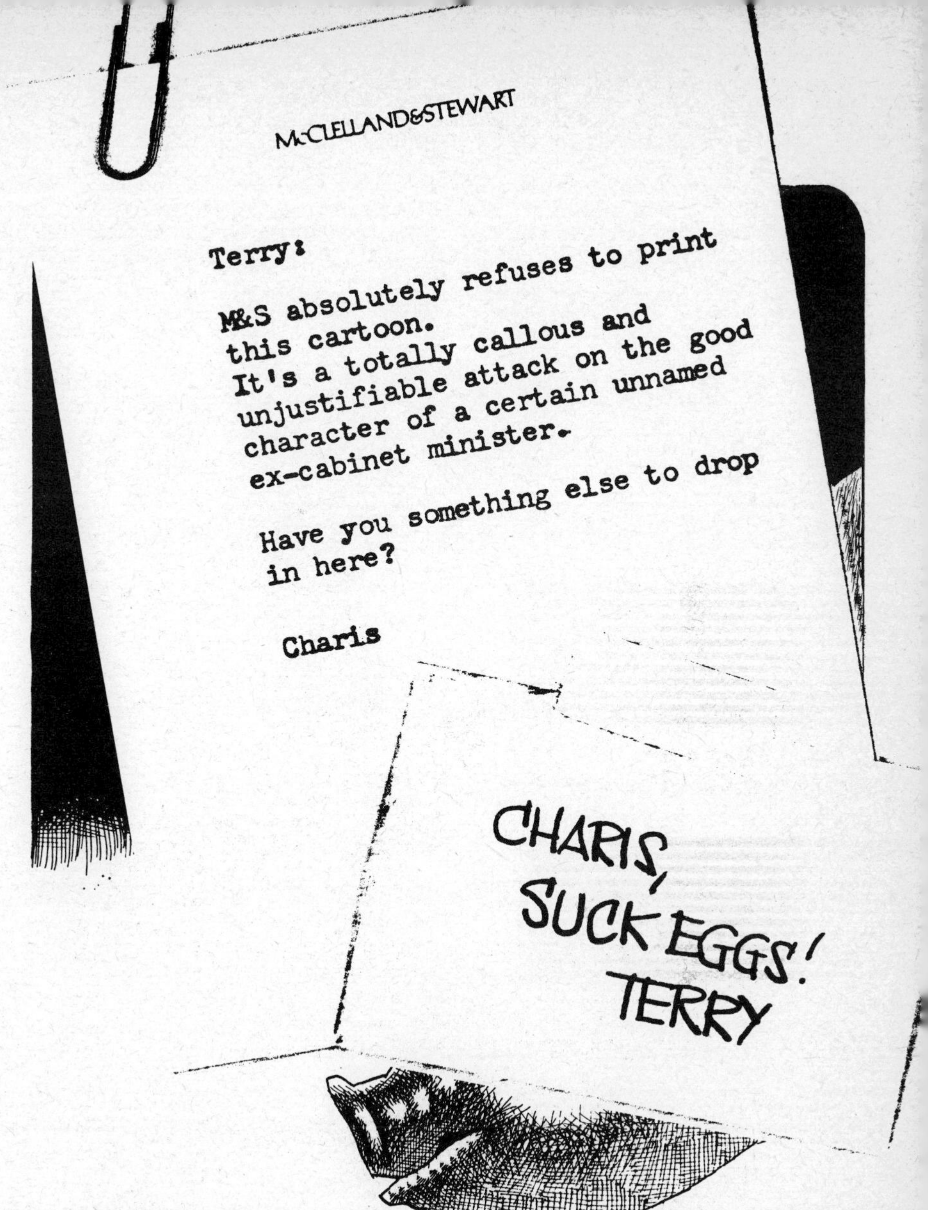
McCLELLAND&STEWART
Terry:
M&S absolutely refuses to print this cartoon.
It's a totally callous and unjustifiable attack on the good character of a certain unnamed ex-cabinet minister.
Have you something else to drop in here?
Charis
CHARIS, SUCK EGGS! TERRY
AISLIN 85
UNPUBLISHED.

ITEM: GOVERNMENT TO PAY SINC STEVENS' LAWYERS $350,000.00!

"COME, COME YOUR HONOR, IF MY PRIME MINISTER ONLY KNEW OF THIS MATTER, HE'D SURELY COVER MY $184. IN PARKING TICKETS AND THE PALTRY $50. FOR MY LAWYER!"

NEWS ITEM: BUTLER AND MAID TAKEN ON MULDOON'S ASIAN TOUR.
AIDE CLAIMS THEIR MAIN JOB WAS SECURITY...
AISLIN '86.
MONTREAL GAZETTE.

THE REAL CONFLICT OF INTEREST HERE WAS STEVENS' BUMPING MY ORIENTAL EXPEDITION OFF THE FRONT PAGE EVERY DAY!!:
SING SUNK!
ACCEPTED
AISLIN 86. MONTREAL GAZETTE

AISLIN 86 MONTREAL GAZETTE
BRIAN?! WELCOME HOME!
TORY HEADQUARTERS

HEH, HEH... JUST A HOBBY...
ONLY $300. EACH!!
GET'EM HERE... CHRIST COINS!
AISLIN 86
MONTREAL GAZETTE

...SINC WHO?..
MULDOO
INC.
AISLIN 86
MONTREAL GAZETTE

⇨ THE U.S. AND US...

...REGARDING ACID RAIN...
AISLIN 86
MONTREAL GAZETTE

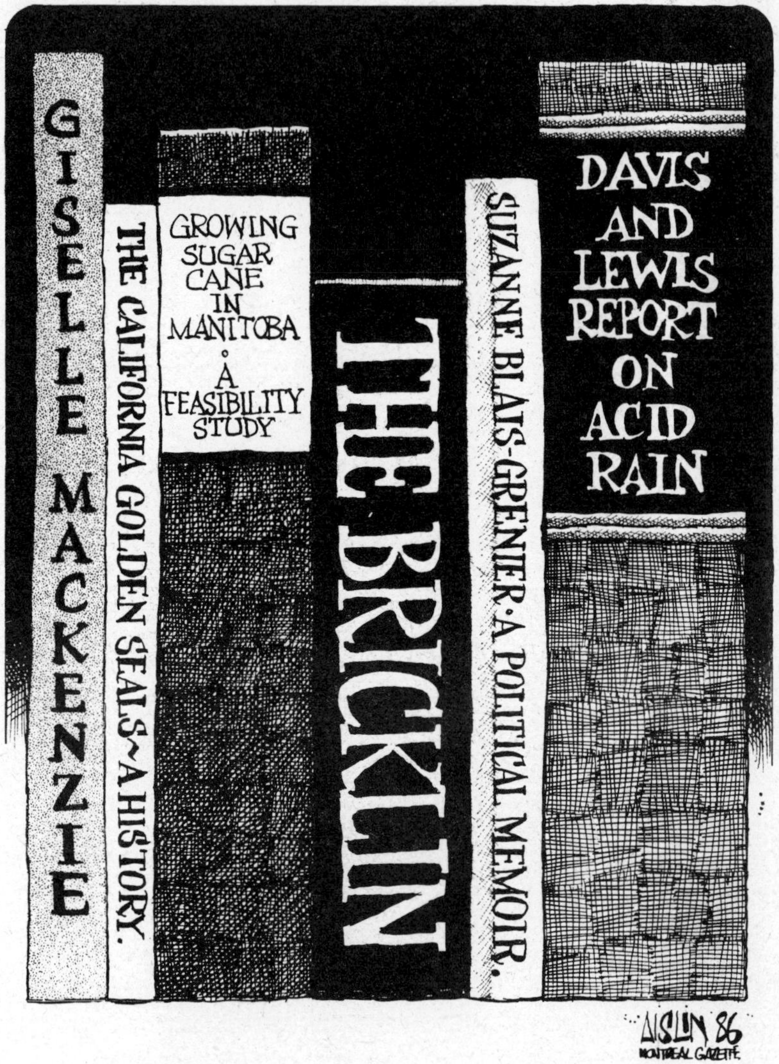
GISELLE MACKENZIE
THE CALIFORNIA GOLDEN SEALS~A HISTORY.
GROWING SUGAR CANE IN MANITOBA A FEASIBILITY STUDY
THE BRICKLIN
SUZANNE BLAIS-GRENIER·A POLITICAL MEMOIR.
DAVIS AND LEWIS REPORT ON ACID RAIN
AISLIN 86
MONTREAL GAZETTE

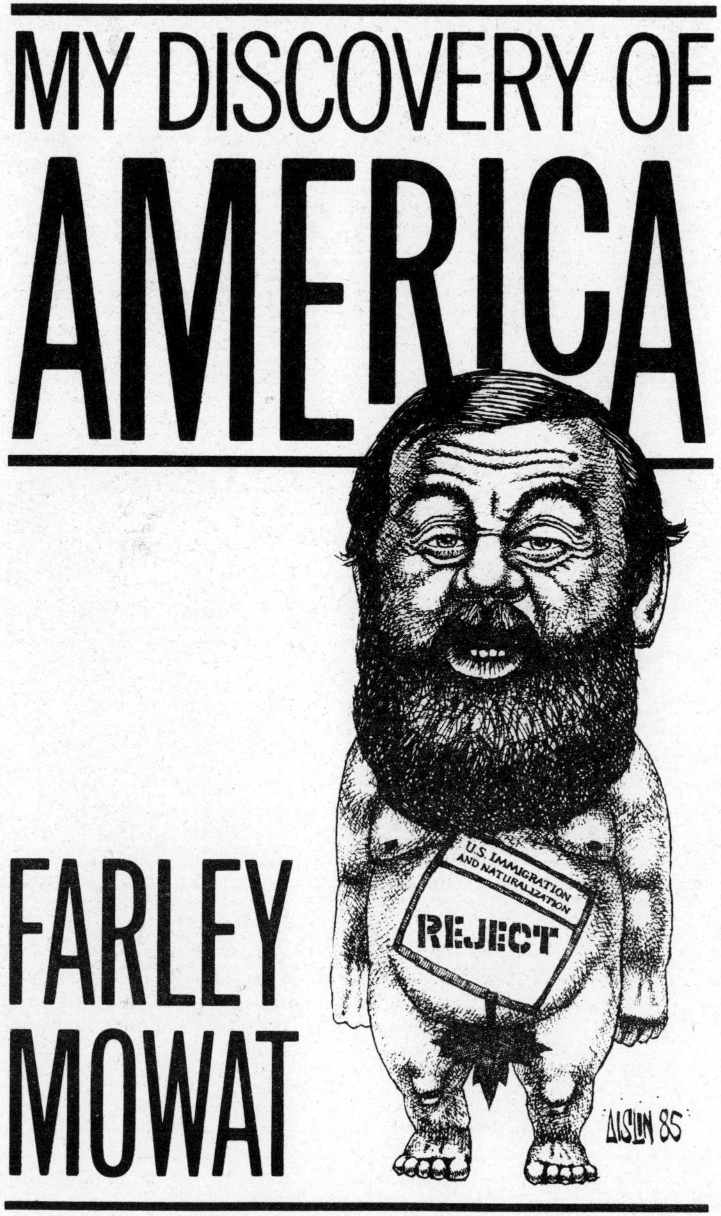
MY DISCOVERY OF
AMERICA
U.S. IMMIGRATION AND NATURALIZATION
REJECT
FARLEY
MOWAT
AISLIN 85

...IN THIS CORNER,*SONDRA!!
AISLIN 86
MONTREAL GAZETTE
*MRS. GOTLIEB'S WARDROBE COURTESY OF CANADIAN TIRE.

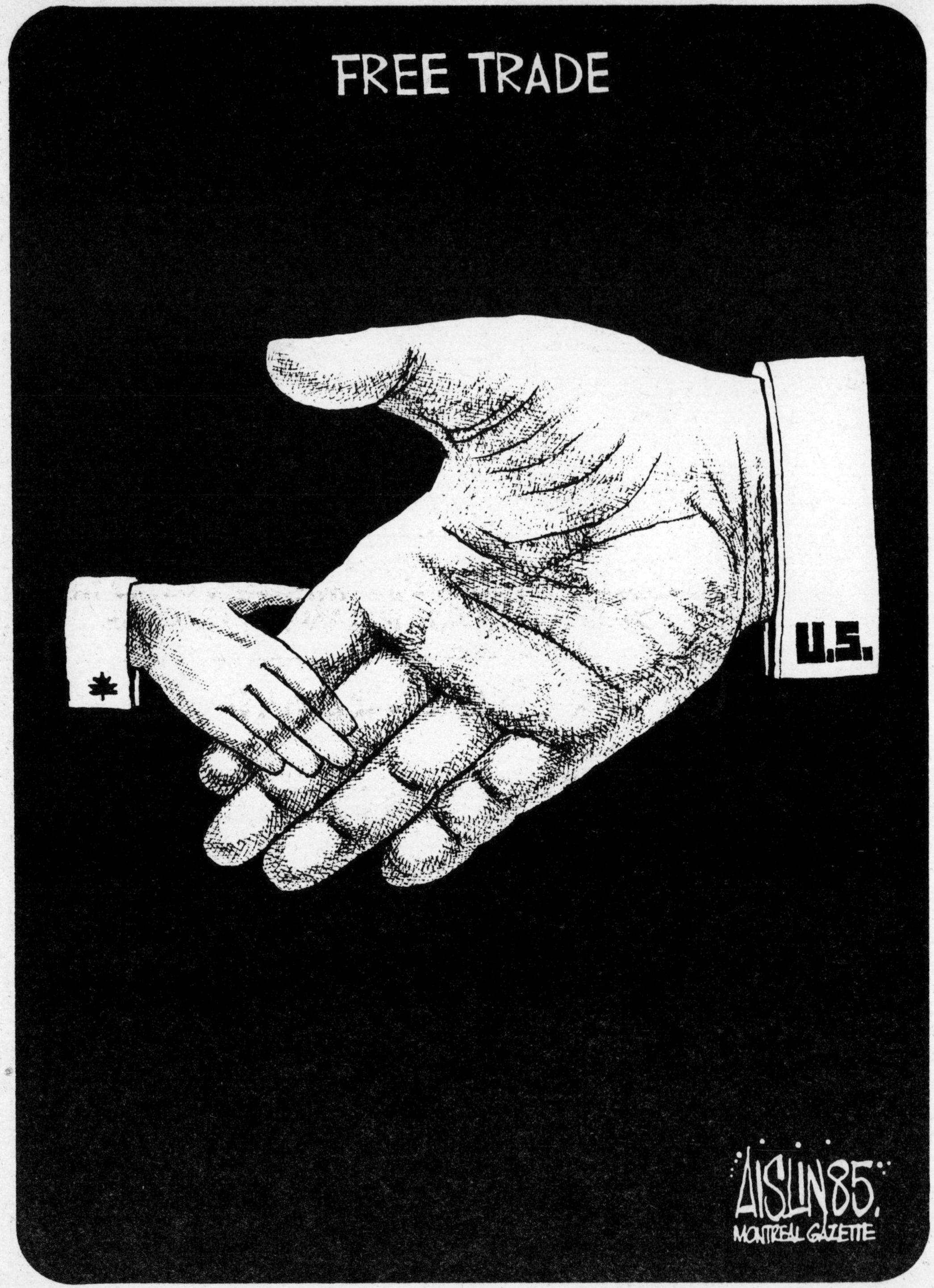
FREE TRADE
U.S.
AISLIN 85
MONTREAL GAZETTE

BLACKJACK, YOU SAY... WHAT'S THAT, SON? SOME SORT OF GAME?
AISLIN 86
MTL GAZETTE

"...OUR UNIQUE CULTURAL IDENTITY..."
BRIAN MULRONEY.
PUCK
CULTURE
AISLIN 85.
MONTREAL GAZETTE

THE U.S. MUST KNOW THAT SOME THINGS ARE SACRED AND ARE NOT ON THE FREE TRADE TABLE! LIKE...
1 THE ARCTIC.
WHERE ELSE CAN WE GO IF BOTH OUR NEIGHBOURS (NOT NEIGHBORS) COMMENCE DROPPING THE BIG ONES?
2 THE N.D.P.
REMEMBER, SOME YANKS THOUGHT PIERRE TRUDEAU WAS A TROTSKYITE... SO THEY'D PROBABLY GIVE THE N.D.P. TO THE N.R.A. FOR TARGET PRACTICE...
3
EH?
THE U.S. CAN KEEP "HAVE A GOOD DAY" + "HI, Y'ALL!" WE'LL HOLD ON TO OUR FAVORITE INTERJECTION!!
4 THE R.C.M.P.
CAN YOU PICTURE OUR GUYS APPEARING ON "MIAMI VICE" IN ALL THOSE PINKS AND YELLOWS AND BABY BLUES??? ALWAYS GETTING THEIR WOMAN? NAH...
AISLIN 86.
MONTREAL GAZETTE.

"THAT'S RIGHT – CANADIAN TELEVISION – ASKING AVERAGE AMERICANS HOW YOU VIEW THE PROGRESS OF THE SIMON REISMAN – PETER MURPHY TALKS??"
AISLIN 86
MONTREAL GAZETTE

CANADA
CURLING
MOOSE JAW
R.C.M.P.
70¢
WAYNE
FRONT PAGE CHALLENGE
POUTINE
A.Y. JACKSON
RICHARD HATFIELD
MACLEAN'S
VALDY
BRIAN
6:30 IN NEWFOUNDLAND
AIR CANADA
WATER
N.W.T.
RYE
N.D.P.
C.F.L.
EH?
6/49
CN
PETER MURPHY
BUTCHER
AISLIN 87
MONTREAL GAZETTE

FREE
TRADE
...A LITTLE
HIGHER,
RON...
AISLIN 86.
MTL. GAZETTE.

AGAINST FREE TRADE
-RAY.
-LIBERAL-LEFT.
-PROFESSIONAL.
-ETHNIC BACKGROUND.
-MASTERCARD.
-MAZDA.
-C.B.C.
-MACLEAN'S.
-EXPOS.
-SCOTCH or WINE (WHITE).
-JANE FONDA.
-PASTA.
-WORRIED THAT FREE TRADE MIGHT ELIMINATE HIS JOB.
FOR FREE TRADE
-ANDREW.
-TORY.
-BUSINESSMAN.
-WASP.
-AMERICAN EXPRESS.
-BUICK.
-C.T.V.
-FINANCIAL POST.
-BLUE JAYS.
-RYE AND DIET PEPSI.
-DOLLY PARTON.
-BEEF.
-ISN'T WORRIED ABOUT FREE TRADE ELIMINATING RAY'S JOB.
AISLIN 87.
MONTREAL GAZETTE.

·P.M. "SCOLDS" GEORGE BUSH DURING OTTAWA VISIT.

MERCI, JEAN...
AISLIN 86
MONTREAL GAZETTE

· STORE SCUFFLE WITH COP AND CIVILIAN FILMED ON VIDEO.

· WELFARE RECIPIENTS SPLIT LOTTERY WINNINGS.

⇨ NICK...

·NICK <u>DOESN'T</u> RUN IN PROVINCIAL ELECTION!

HAVE A DRINK WITH ~~A COMMUNIST~~, ~~SEPARATIST~~, ~~SOCIAL DEMOCRAT~~, ~~SMALL 'L' LIBERAL~~, ~~FEDERALIST~~, ~~TORY~~, ~~BRING BACK THE NOOSER~~, MELISSA'S DAD...

$50.00 CASA PEDRO
TUESDAY JUNE 3d
7 P.M. TIL NOD OUT.

·POSTER FOR AUF DER MAUR FUND-RAISER.

·NICK DETAINED BY MONTREAL'S FINEST.

SOON CONDO!!

·PHYLLIS LAMBERT.
AISLIN 87.

fermé
closed

AISLIN 86
MONTREAL GAZETTE

·EVERYONE SHOWS UP FOR STANLEY CUP RIOT EXCEPT THE POLICE.

·JEAN DRAPEAU CAMPAIGNS FOR HIS SUCCESSOR CLAUDE DUPRAS.

·POLLS OVERWHELMINGLY FAVOR JEAN DORÉ.

·JEAN DRAPEAU RETIRES.

THE REMEMBRANCE DAY CEREMONIES ARE DOWN THE STREET—THIS IS A SMALL MEMORIAL FOR THE CIVIC PARTY...
AISLIN 86
MONTREAL GAZETTE.

· PARTY FOR EX-MONTREALERS LIVING IN TORONTO IS A COMPLETE BUST.

"HOLY COW, MARG, IT'S 10:25! WE DON'T WANT TO MISS OUR GO TRAIN..."

·BUS DRIVERS MAY STRIKE.

QUÉBEC.

NOVEMBER 15, 1976...
NOUS VOULONS LA RÉVOLUTION À L'INTÉRIEUR DU SYSTÈME! MAINTENANT QUE NOUS CONTRÔLONS LE GOUVERNEMENT NOUS POLITISERONS LE STATU QUO ET FERONS DE NOS ENFANTS UNE NOUVELLE GÉNÉRATION DE PATRIOTES...
NOVEMBER 15, 1986...
JE VEUX UN NOUVEAU SYSTÈME RÉVOLUTIONNAIRE! UNE CHAÎNE STÉRÉO BANG & OLUFSEN AVEC DISQUE AU LASER ET CONTRÔLE À DISTANCE; UNE TÉLÉVISION EN STÉRÉO AVEC ENREGISTREMENT NUMÉRIQUE POUR MA B.M.W...
AISLIN 86
MONTREAL GAZETTE

·RENÉ LÉVESQUE RETIRES.

...IT WILL BE NO EASY JOB, FILLING RENÉ LÉVESQUE'S TINY WALLABEES.
AISLIN 85
MONTREAL GAZETTE

·P.Q. ACCOMMODATES HYUNDAI ON LANGUAGE·

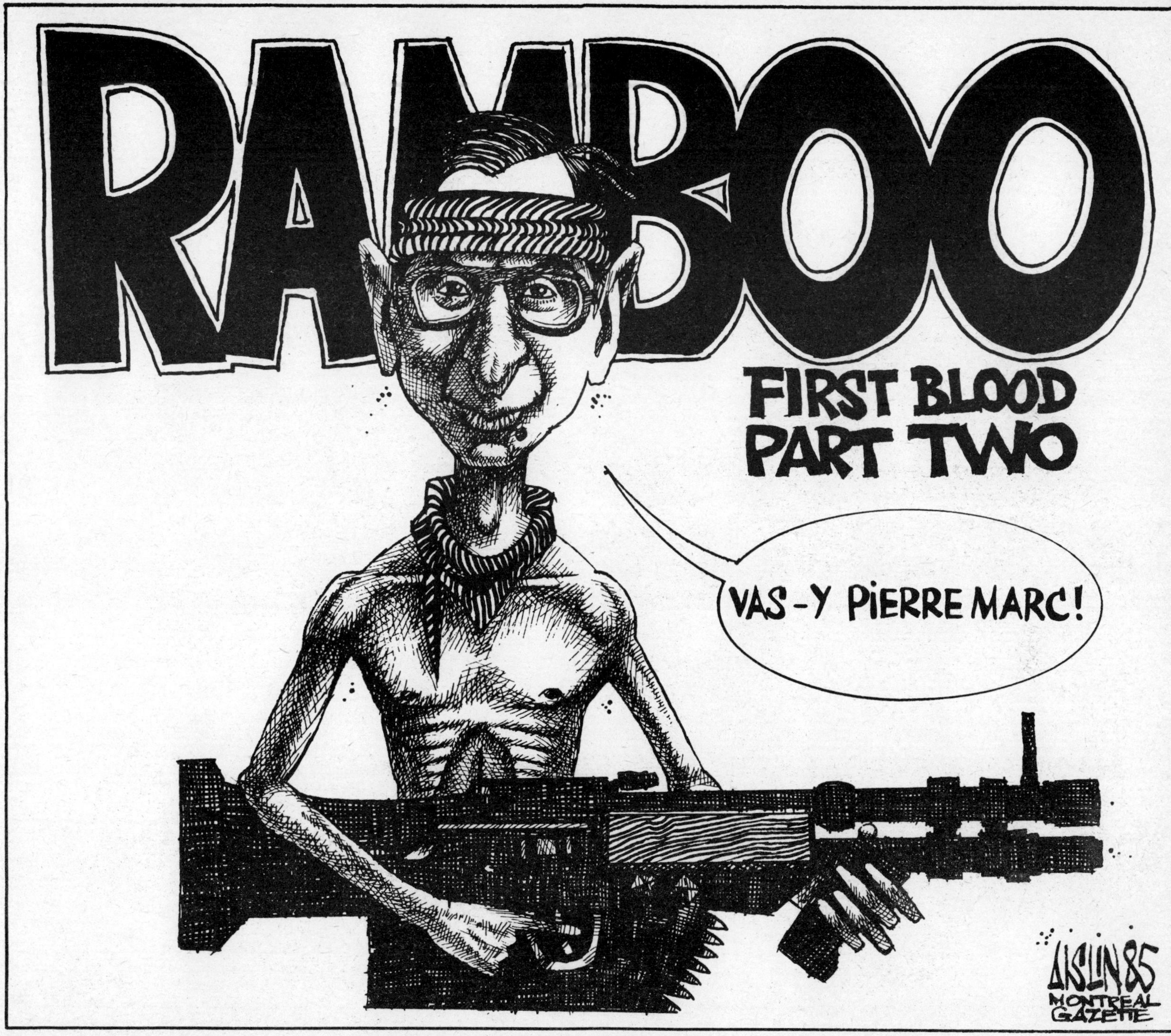
RAMBOO
FIRST BLOOD
PART TWO
VAS-Y PIERRE MARC!
AISLIN 85
MONTREAL GAZETTE

ZZZZ...
WAKE UP, MICHEL.
WHAT IS IT, JOAN?
DO YOU REALIZE THAT WITHIN 48 HOURS WE'LL HAVE TO DECIDE WHETHER WE'RE VOTING FOR BOURASSA OR JOHNSON?
YES...
ZZZ...
ZZ...
AISLIN 85
MONTREAL GAZETTE

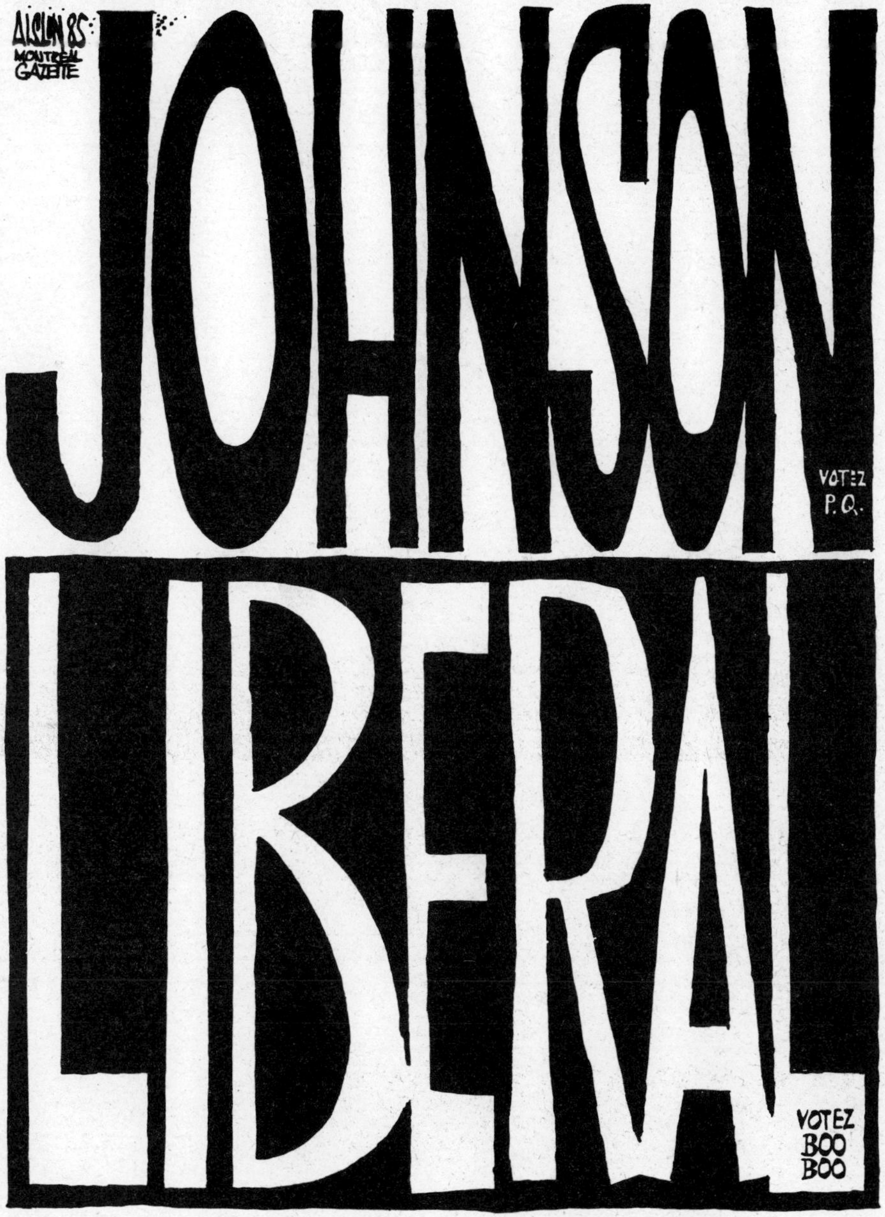

·AFTER 10 YEAR ABSENCE, BOURASSA RE-ELECTED.

·QUEBEC'S NEW WELFARE POLICE·

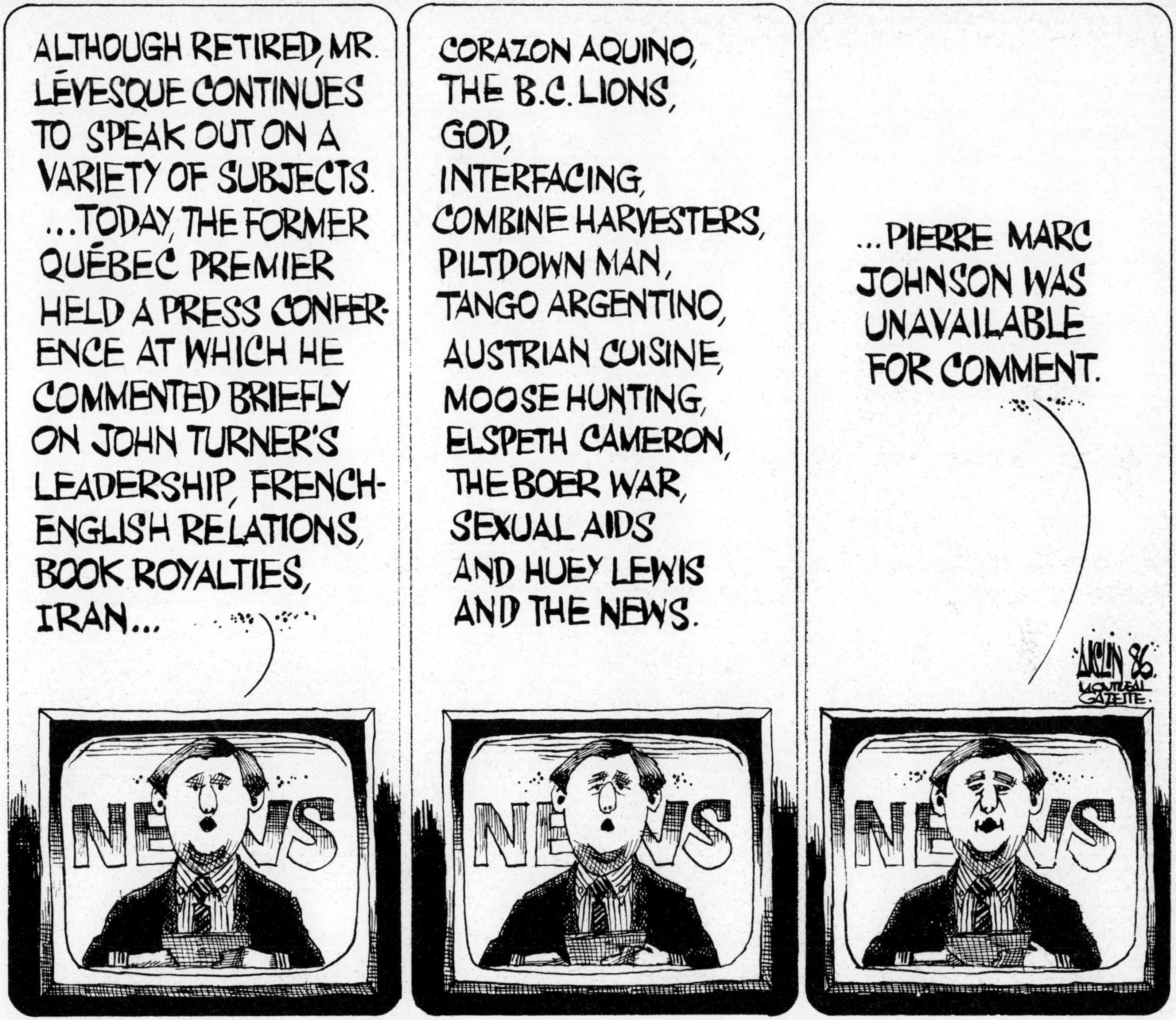
ALTHOUGH RETIRED, MR. LÉVESQUE CONTINUES TO SPEAK OUT ON A VARIETY OF SUBJECTS. ...TODAY, THE FORMER QUÉBEC PREMIER HELD A PRESS CONFERENCE AT WHICH HE COMMENTED BRIEFLY ON JOHN TURNER'S LEADERSHIP, FRENCH-ENGLISH RELATIONS, BOOK ROYALTIES, IRAN...
NEWS
CORAZON AQUINO, THE B.C. LIONS, GOD, INTERFACING, COMBINE HARVESTERS, PILTDOWN MAN, TANGO ARGENTINO, AUSTRIAN CUISINE, MOOSE HUNTING, ELSPETH CAMERON, THE BOER WAR, SEXUAL AIDS AND HUEY LEWIS AND THE NEWS.
NEWS
...PIERRE MARC JOHNSON WAS UNAVAILABLE FOR COMMENT.
AISLIN 86. MONTREAL GAZETTE.
NEWS

· TWO QUEBEC LADIES IN ROME SUSPECTED OF DOPE SMUGGLING!

ARVIDA VICE!

GILLES RHÉAUME...
TI-BEC
AISLIN 86
MONTREAL GAZETTE

HALLELUJAH! FINALLY QUÉBEC IS GOING TO ENSHRINE ENGLISH LANGUAGE RIGHTS!!
...NOW THAT WE'RE ENSCONCED HERE IN ETOBICOKE.
AISLIN 85
MONTREAL GAZETTE

ITEM: BILL 101 SUPPORTERS TO TOUR WEST END HUNTING ENGLISH SIGNS.
MINUTE... BLAIS-GRENIER VEUT UNE LIMOUSINE.
ET PIERRE MARC VEUT QU'ON S'ARRÊTE CHEZ HOLT-RENFREW.
ET PUIS VIGNEAULT VEUT ALLER CHEZ SAM'S!
ENSUITE RHÉAUME VEUT ARRÊTER AU ROSE BOWL.
HÉ... OÙ EST LAURIN?
AVEC BRIAN...
ILS SONT ALLER CHERCHER MILA CHEZ CHARLES OF WESTMOUNT.
AUTOBUS SCOLAIRE
AISLIN 86

·QUEBEC GOVT. SLOW TO GUARANTEE BILINGUAL RIGHTS.

UNPUBLISHED.

SORRY, BUB... NOBODY SAID ANYTHING TO ME ABOUT PAINTING HER UP IN FRENCH... ANYWAYS, IT LOSES IN TRANSLATION.

FEAR...
GRRRRR!!
CLICK! CLICK! CLICK! CLICK! CLICK!
I WONDER IF WINOS USE GEL?
HEY, I'M A FEMINIST, BABE!
BEWARE! RABID HEATHEN.
Eh, Eh?

AND LOATHING...

·CONTINUAL SHUTTLE PROBLEMS.

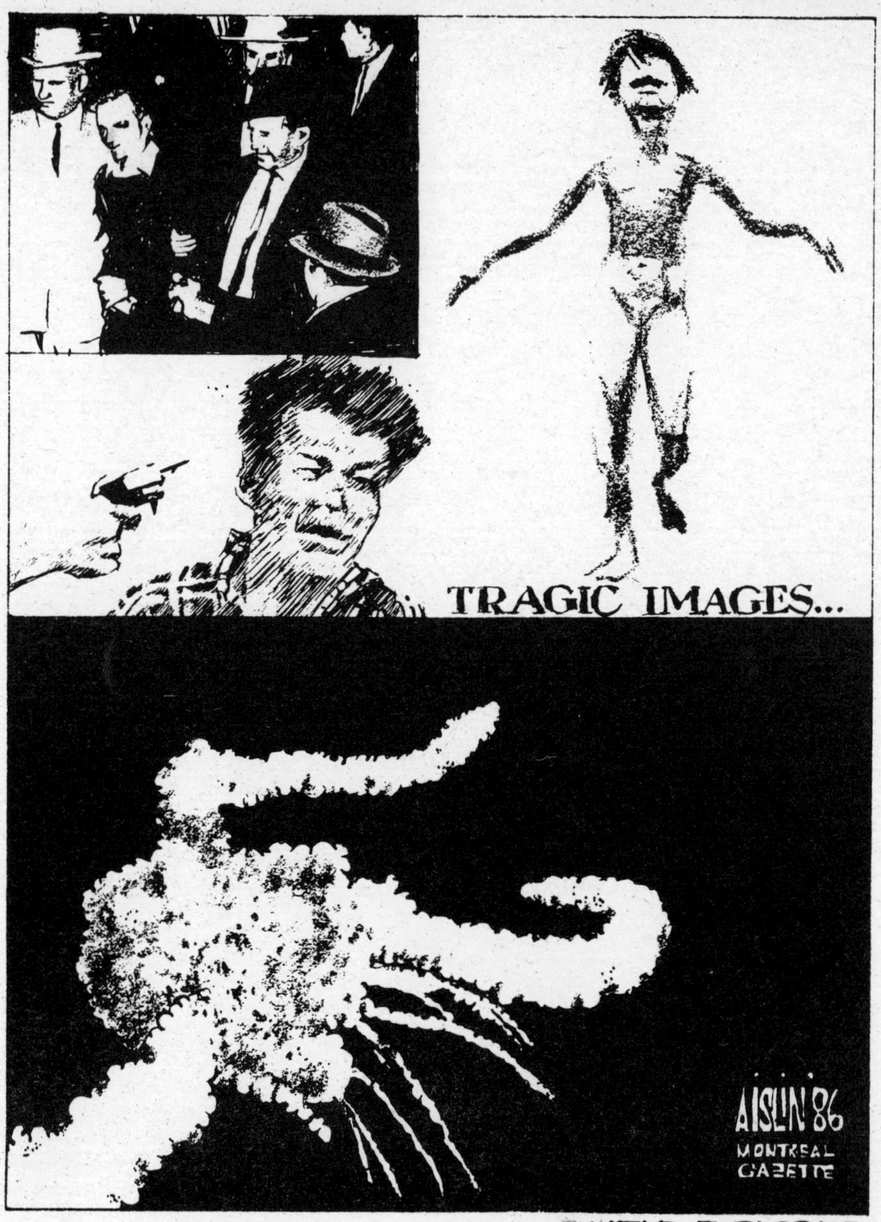

·SHUTTLE EXPLODES.

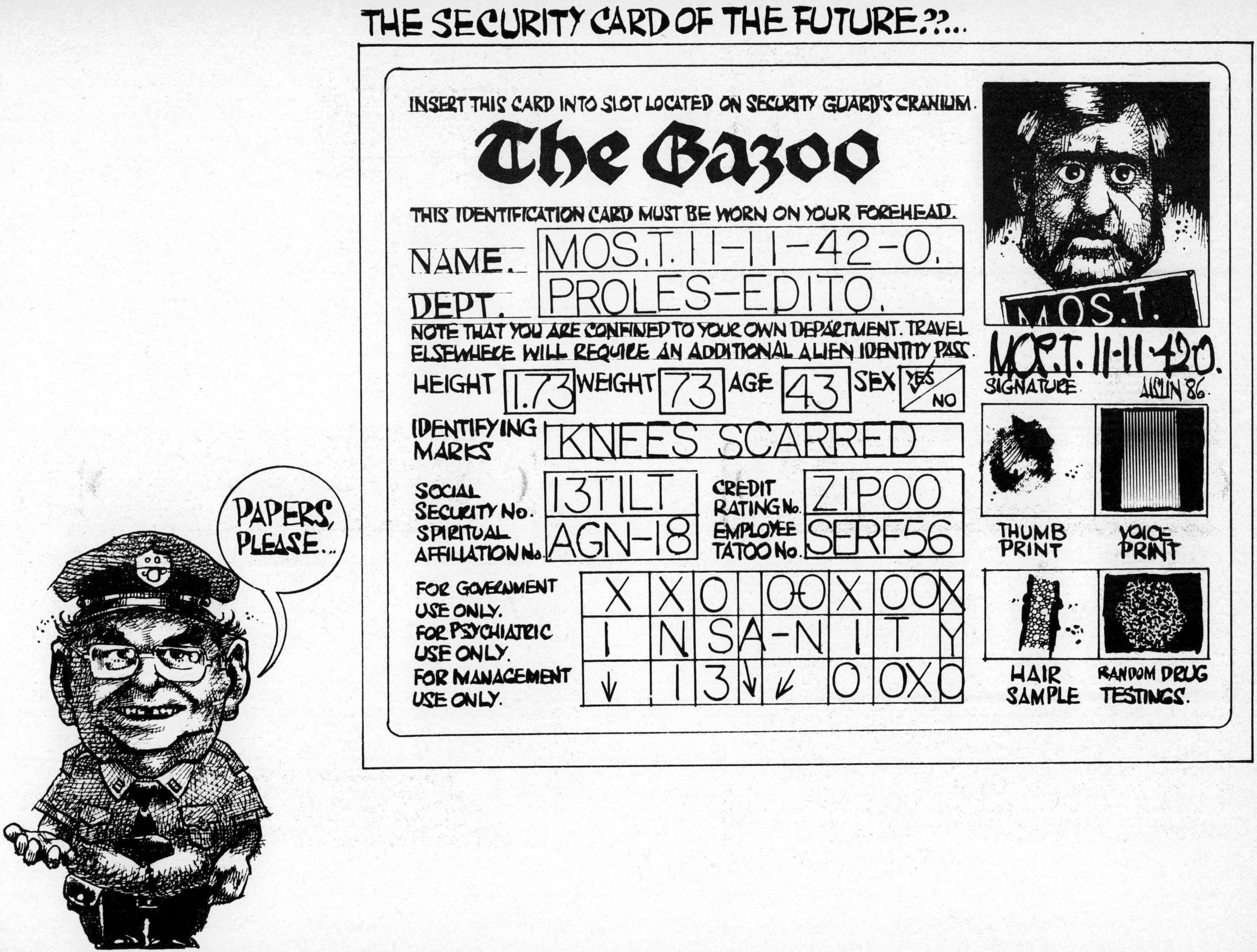
THE SECURITY CARD OF THE FUTURE??...
INSERT THIS CARD INTO SLOT LOCATED ON SECURITY GUARD'S CRANIUM.
The Gazoo
THIS IDENTIFICATION CARD MUST BE WORN ON YOUR FOREHEAD.
NAME. MOS.T. 11-11-42-0.
DEPT. PROLES-EDITO.
NOTE THAT YOU ARE CONFINED TO YOUR OWN DEPARTMENT. TRAVEL ELSEWHERE WILL REQUIRE AN ADDITIONAL ALIEN IDENTITY PASS.
HEIGHT 1.73 WEIGHT 73 AGE 43 SEX YES NO
IDENTIFYING MARKS KNEES SCARRED
SOCIAL SECURITY No. 13TILT
SPIRITUAL AFFILIATION No. AGN-18
CREDIT RATING No. ZIP00
EMPLOYEE TATOO No. SERF56
FOR GOVERNMENT USE ONLY. X X O OO X OO X
FOR PSYCHIATRIC USE ONLY. I N SA-N I T Y
FOR MANAGEMENT USE ONLY. 1 3 0 0X0
MOS.T.
MOS.T. 11-11-420.
SIGNATURE
AISLIN '86.
THUMB PRINT
VOICE PRINT
HAIR SAMPLE
RANDOM DRUG TESTINGS.
PAPERS, PLEASE...

·ENGLISH FOOTBALL.

·PARIS BOMBINGS

·THANKSGIVING·

METAL DETECTOR
ZZZZZZZ
AISLIN '85
MONTREAL GAZETTE
WELL, SON, I SURE HOPE YOU'RE WEARING METAL TEETH OR YOU ATE A HUB CAP FOR LUNCH. OTHERWISE IT'S JUST YOU AND MS. CRUNCHIT IN THE BACK ROOM...

IRONIC, AIN'T IT, EVERY AIRPORT IN THE WESTERN WORLD STARTING TO LOOK JUST LIKE TRIPOLI'S?
AISLIN 86
MONTREAL GAZETTE

· EUROPEANS SLOW TO CRITICIZE LIBYA.

UNPUBLISHED.

·REAGAN CALLS GADHAFI MAD DOG.

AISLIN 87
MONTREAL GAZETTE
...OH, I KNOW, I KNOW, MS. REEBOK... WE'RE HEALTHIER AND WILL LIVE MUCH LONGER—BUT WHY DO SMOKERS ALWAYS LOOK SO MUCH MORE INTERESTING?

SIR!! NO SMOKING ON THIS FLIGHT!!
TNT
AISLIN 86.
MONTREAL GAZETTE

1940's
50's
60's
70's
80's
90's
CONDOMS
AISLIN 87.
MONTREAL GAZETTE

FOR YOUR ETERNAL BEAUTY, DOTH MY LOVE EVER INSPIRE, TO FLOWER FORTH...
...VERY ROMANTIC, RANDOLPH... BUT, DID YOU REMEMBER THE CONDOMS?
AISLIN 87
MONTREAL GAZETTE.

MY! MY! MY! WHAT HAVE WE HERE? ROOM 2209...TWO OYSTER STEW...A 1961 CHÂTEAU PÉTRUS...AND SIXTEEN RIBBED RAMSES...
NEWS ITEM
MONTREAL HOTEL WILL GIVE AWAY CONDOMS.
AISLIN 87
MONTREAL GAZETTE

ITEM: SEVENTY-TWO DEFENCELESS HINDU MEN, WOMEN, CHILDREN SLAUGHTERED BY "THE KHALISTAN COMMANDO FORCE."
AISLIN 87
MONTREAL GAZETTE
THE COWARDS.

WE'LL JUST HAVE TO PUT IRAN AND NICARAGUA ON THE BACK BURNER WHILE WE DEAL WITH REAL PROBLEMS... LIKE NANCY'S HAIRDRESSER. HE GIVES ME SOME GUCK THAT KEEPS MY HAIR RIGIDLY IN PLACE... WE'RE HOPING HE'LL HAVE SOMETHING FOR MY NECK...
AISLIN 86
MONTREAL GAZETTE

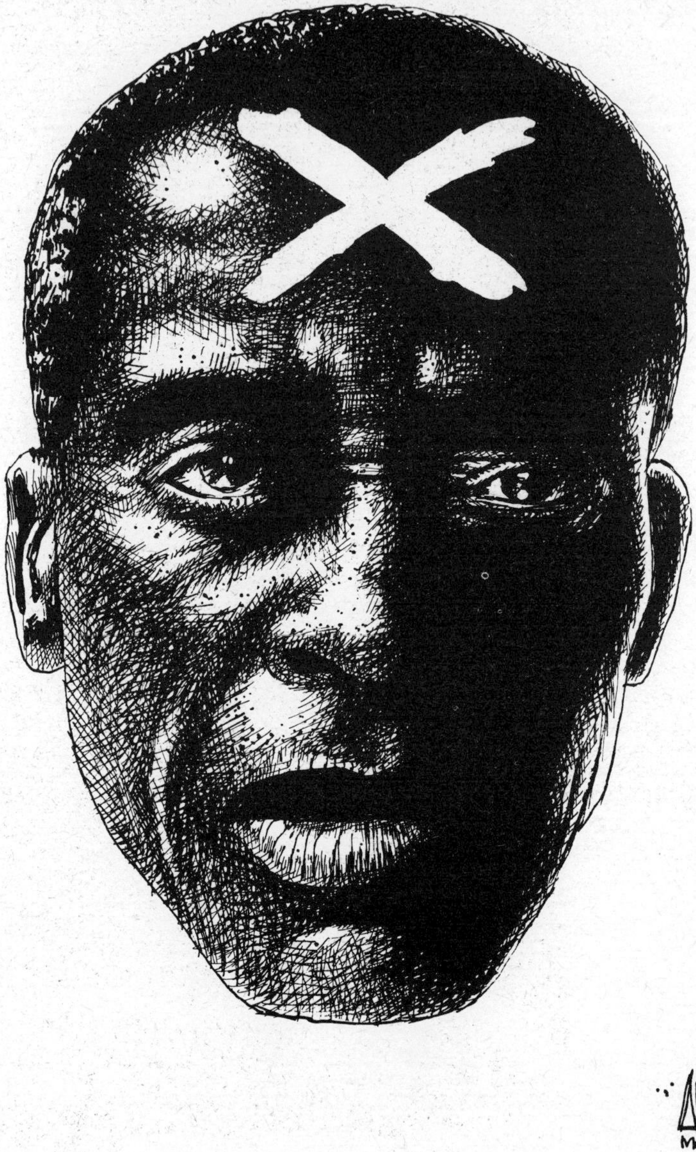

·WHITE-ONLY SOUTH AFRICAN ELECTIONS.

SANCTIONS WOULD BE BAD FOR BLACKS...
AISLIN 86
MONTREAL GAZETTE

-TUTU VISITS TORONTO, MONTREAL.

BOTHA
AISLIN 85.
MONTREAL GAZETTE

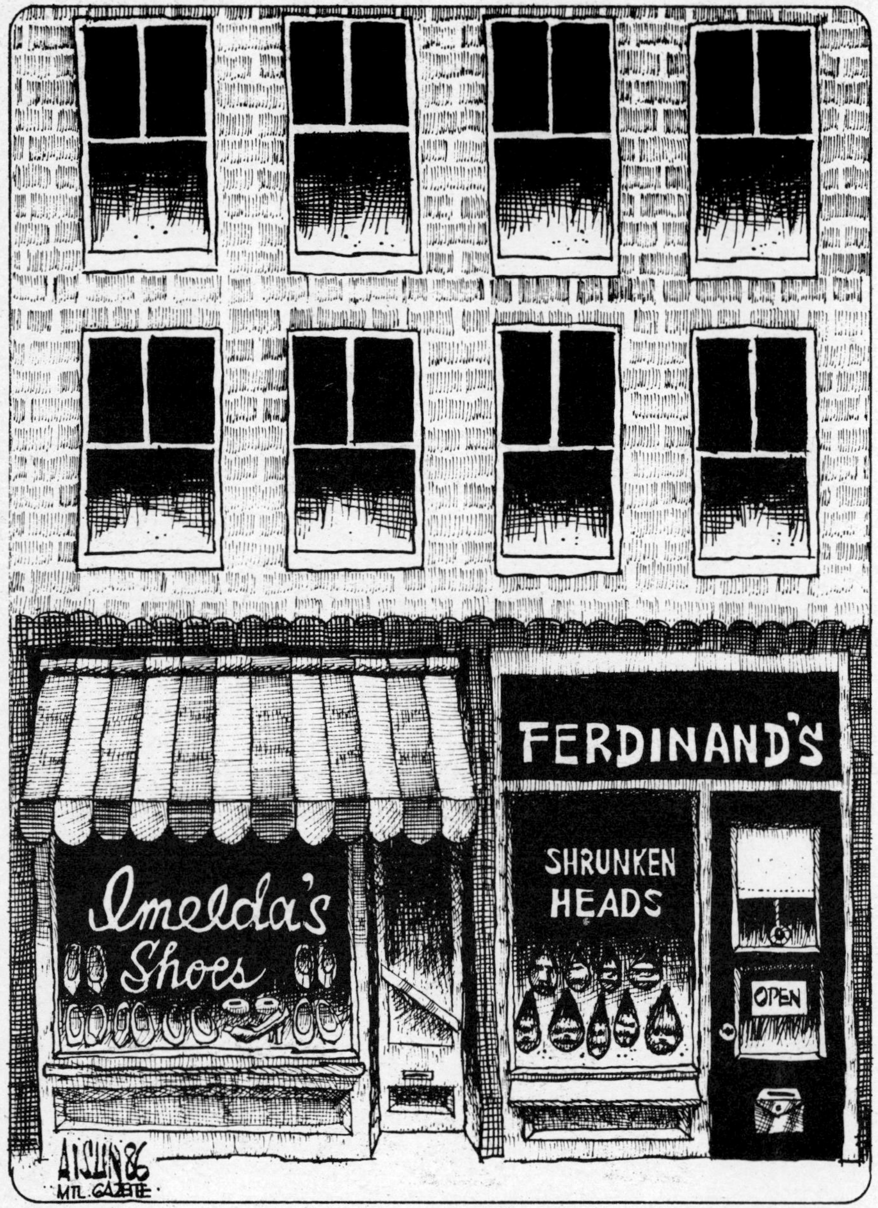
FERDINAND'S
SHRUNKEN HEADS
OPEN
Imelda's Shoes
AISLIN 86
MTL. GAZETTE

YOU TOO CAN HELP! SUPPORT THIS FUN THIRD WORLD COUPLE! A MERE SEVERAL HUNDRED MILLION A YEAR WILL KEEP THEM IN A STYLE TO WHICH THEY'VE BECOME ACCUSTOMED... MAKE ALL MONIES PAYABLE TO:
ADOPT A DICTATOR.
AISLIN 86
MONTREAL GAZETTE
"BABY DOC"
"BABY DUCK"

PSST...
MAYDAY...
MAYDAY...
AISLIN 86.
MONTREAL GAZETTE

-CHERNOBYL.

TELEGRAM
RUSSIAN P.O.W.'s
AFGHANISTAN.
CAN YOU PLAY HOCKEY?
JOE CLARK.
AISLIN 86.
MONTREAL GAZETTE

AISLIN 87
MONTREAL GAZETTE
AFGHANISTAN

AISLIN 87
MONTREAL GAZETTE

· GLASNOST.

·THATCHER ELECTED TO THIRD TERM.
DENIS AND I...
AISLIN 87
MONTREAL GAZETTE.

OPENING SOON!!
THE THING FROM B.C!!
STARRING BILL VANDER ZALM
AISLIN 86.
MTL GAZETTE

NEWS ITEM: MORE DEMANDS THAT HATFIELD RESIGN.
BROWNIES
WHY?
COOKIES
AISLIN 85
MONTREAL GAZETTE

I…I-UH..I…IT WAS A MISTAKE! I…I…WE…I …THEY… IRANAMUCK.
AISLIN 87 MONTREAL GAZETTE

NATIONAL SECRETARY'S WEEK? IS IT, MR. FERGUSON?... FLOWERS? SURE!! BE A GOOD BOY AND ORDER YOURSELF SOME...
AISLIN 86
MONTREAL GAZETTE

...NOW SAY, "HI THERE," IN A VIGOROUS AND VIRILE MANNER, RON.
HI, THERE, IN A VIGOROUS AND VIRILE MANNER, RON!!!
AISLIN 87
MONTREAL GAZETTE

NO, THERE'S NOTHING TO WORRY ABOUT, LADY... WE'VE BEEN SEEING ALOT OF THIS RECENTLY - OLD WATERGATE JUNKIES SUDDENLY GOING INTO A EUPHORIC TRANCE.
M.D.
COVERUP?
LIES?
AISLIN 86
MONTREAL GAZETTE

VIDEO PLUS
RAMBO
PART II
THE TERMINATOR
DEATH WISH 3
À VENIR!
COMING SOON!
LORTIE!
AISLIN 87.

HMMM...
THE CHIMNEY'S
STONEWALLED...
WHITE
HOUSE
AISLIN 86
MONTREAL
GAZETTE

-CONVENIENCE STORE KILLINGS.

"...OTHERWISE, MRS. BUBBLEFORK, NOTHING HAS CHANGED. YOU STILL CAN FIND YOUR 'PREPARATION H' ON AISLE TWO, BOTTOM SHELF..."

"...WELL, LORD, I DON'T NEED NO $8 MILLION—JUST A COUPLE OF HUNDRED TO GET LI'L NORMA-LEE-LINDA-MAY HERE OUTTA TOWN.!!"

Tammy: 'All we've got is $37,000 left'
Jack Kelley
USA TODAY
TEGA CAY, S.C. — A tearful Tammy Bakker said Wednesday she wished new PTL chief Jerry Falwell had "killed me and Jim" rather than make them suffer the agony of losing their ministry.
"I know what it's like to b hunted like a scared anim she said. talkir to re for the tim husba ile i
HOW CAIN AH POSSIBLY BE SAIXY FO' JIM WITH A LI'L OL' $37,000?
THET'S RIGHT... COULD COST 'ER A HALF MILLION.
AISLIN 87
MONTREAL GAZETTE

...IN CLOSING, LET ME SAY TO EACH OF YOU - ORAL, BILLY, JIMMY, JERRY, TAMMY-FAYE AND JIM - HOW MUCH I'VE ENJOYED OUR CONVERSATIONS OVER THE YEARS. INCIDENTALLY, WHEN YOU ARRIVE HERE IN HEAVEN, DO WE HAVE A SURPRISE FOR YOU!
LOVE, GOD.
AISLIN 87
MTL. GAZETTE.

...AND THEN, IF I REMEMBER CORRECTLY, EITHER COLONEL MUSTARD OR PROFESSOR PLUM WAS IN THE CONSERVATORY. MEANWHILE, MISS SCARLET WAS WITH THE WRENCH IN THE LIBRARY...
AISLIN 87
MONTREAL GAZETTE

"BRAZIL HAS STOPPED MAKING LOAN PAYMENTS...ECUADOR HAS STOPPED MAKING LOAN PAYMENTS...SO, REGARDING MY MONTHLY PAYMENT OF $205.86? AMIGO, LET ME TELL YOU ABOUT A PLACE WHERE THE SUN DON'T SHINE..."

· ROYAL KIDDIES ACTING UP.

PABLO PICASSO

·HENRY MOORE.

THE TORIES-PART TWO...
...FACE FACTS, DAD, WE TORIES HAVE CHANGED!
GLOBE
MAIL
AISLIN 86
MONTREAL GAZETTE

- ONGOING POSTAL PROBLEMS, RATE INCREASES.

MAY 23d IS AN ANNIVERSARY OF SORTS FOR ME... IT WILL MARK MY THIRD UNEMPLOYED BUDGET...
AISLIN 85 MONTREAL GAZETTE

NEWS ITEM: JEANNE SAUVÉ TO SPEND $600,000.00 ON HER KITCHEN!!!
POT LUCK, CHEZ MOI ...B.Y.O.B.
AISLIN 85 MONTREAL GAZETTE

MICHAEL WILSON SHOES
BUDGET SALE!
RUBBER BOOTS
AISLIN 85
MONTREAL GAZETTE

WELL, YOU HAVE THE AMERICAN DOLLAR AND THE CANADIAN DOLLAR MUCH LIKE YOU HAVE THE CHICAGO BEARS AND THE CALGARY STAMPS!
AISLIN 86
MONTREAL GAZETTE

· FLIGHT ATTENDANT SUSPENDED FOR CRITICIZING TORIES.

- GOVERNMENT REPORT ON PORNOGRAPHY.

"KATE" CARNEY...
GOD BLESS AMERICA!!!
AISLIN 86
MONTREAL GAZETTE

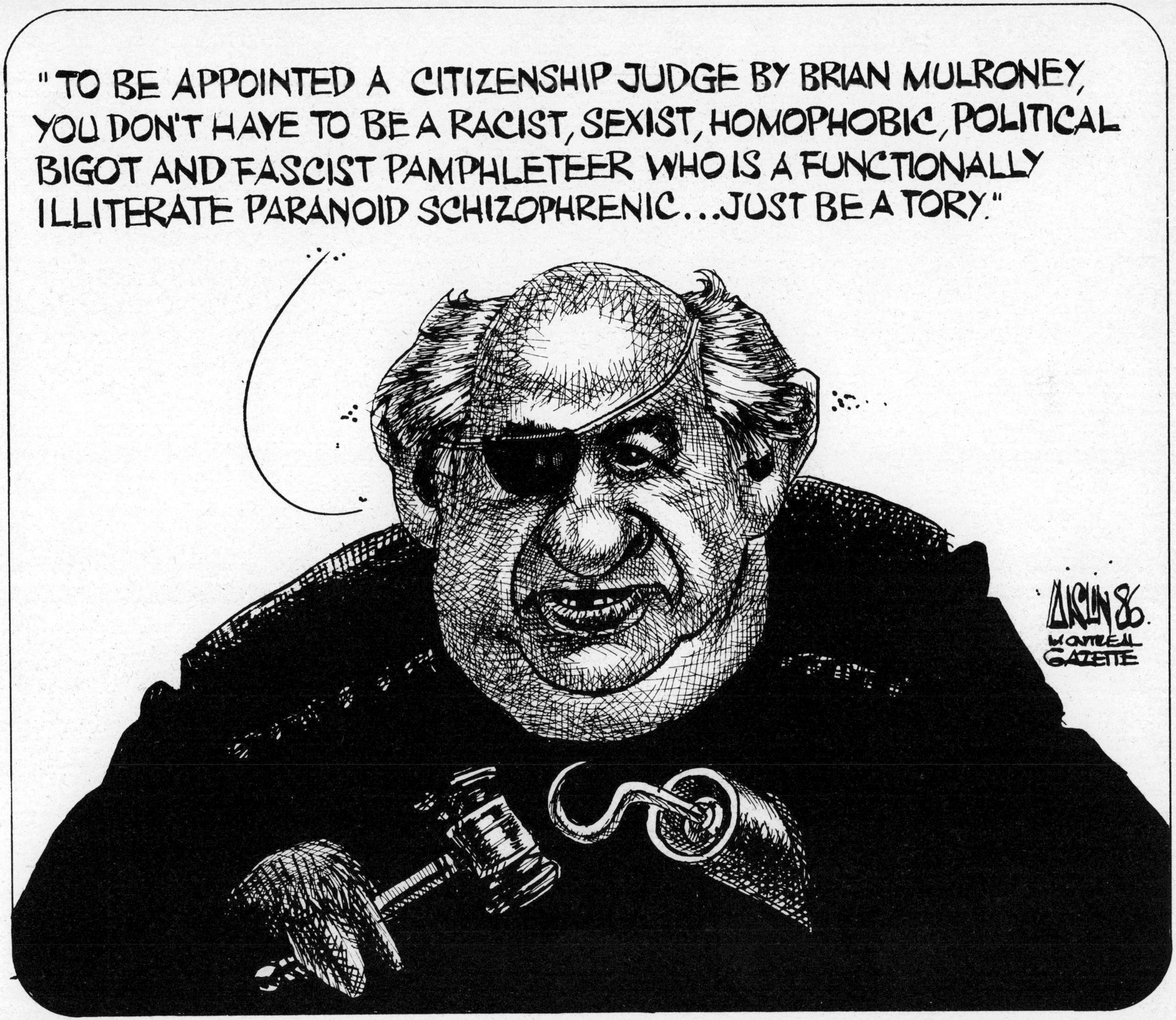
"TO BE APPOINTED A CITIZENSHIP JUDGE BY BRIAN MULRONEY, YOU DON'T HAVE TO BE A RACIST, SEXIST, HOMOPHOBIC, POLITICAL BIGOT AND FASCIST PAMPHLETEER WHO IS A FUNCTIONALLY ILLITERATE PARANOID SCHIZOPHRENIC...JUST BE A TORY."
AISLIN 86.
MONTREAL GAZETTE

P.M.'s HOTEL SUITE $3,400.18
MILA'S CAVIAR
CRACKDOWN ON WELFARE CHEATS
PEAS
AISLIN 86.
MONTREAL GAZETTE.

-P.M. BOASTS ABOUT FIGHTING SEPARATISM.

...ON THE OTHER HAND, YOU TORIES MUST BE HEARTENED BY THE FACT THAT JOE CLARK LOOKED JUST GREAT ALL WEEK.
AISLIN 85
MTL. GAZETTE

THE LINEUP...
IMPORTER?
ENFORCER?
PIMP?
EXTORTIONIST?
TORY?
6'
5'
4'
3'
2'
1'
·OERLIKON SCANDAL BREAKS.

THE OPPOSITION AND THE PRESS...
33rd PARLIAMENT...
AISLIN 86
MONTREAL GAZETTE

- TORIES BUGGED LIBERAL CAUCUS IN 60's.

- HALIFAX LIBERAL CONVENTION.

"FACE FACTS, JOHN.... YOU'RE NO BRUCE SPRINGSTEEN."

IT'S NICE TO SEE THE MEDIA DOING THEIR JOB.
THE OTTAWA CITIZEN BROKE THE STORY ON BOB COATES...
C.B.C.'s FIFTH ESTATE EXPOSED THE TUNA SCANDAL LEADING TO JOHN FRASER'S DEMISE...
THEN SOUTHAM NEWS PRINTED THE GOODS ON BLAIS-GRENIER'S EUROPEAN TRIPS...
WHILE SINC STEVENS RESIGNED AFTER THE LOAN AFFAIR APPEARED IN THE GLOBE + MAIL...
BUT, WHEN ARE THE LIBERALS GOING TO DO SOMETHING??
AISLIN 86
MONTREAL GAZETTE

NOTHING SEEMS TO BE WORKING IN THE TORIES' FAVOR THESE DAYS, EH??
PRESS GALLERY
WELL, THERE ARE A FEW THINGS...
OH... LIKE WHAT?
PRESS GALLERY
SHEILA COPPS AND JOHN NUNZIATA.
AISLIN 86
MONTREAL GAZETTE

NEWS ITEM: P.M. BLAMES PRESS FOR HIS WOES...
"SITTING IN THE CORNER, GETTING CORKED ON TOKAY; STUFFIN' RANCID TUNA INTO TINS ALL DAY!
"OH, WE FOLD UP BANKS AND THE PUBLIC WILL PAY FOR OUR EUROPEAN ROMPS, LIKE OL' BLAIS-GRENIER!!
"LET'S GIVE ALL OUR FRIENDS JOBS, AND CUT OFF THE PENSIONERS, OLÉ! OR CLOSE DOWN A REFINERY, MEDIA, MEDIA, HIP-HIP-HOORAY!!"
PRESS CLUB
AISLIN '86 MONTREAL GAZETTE

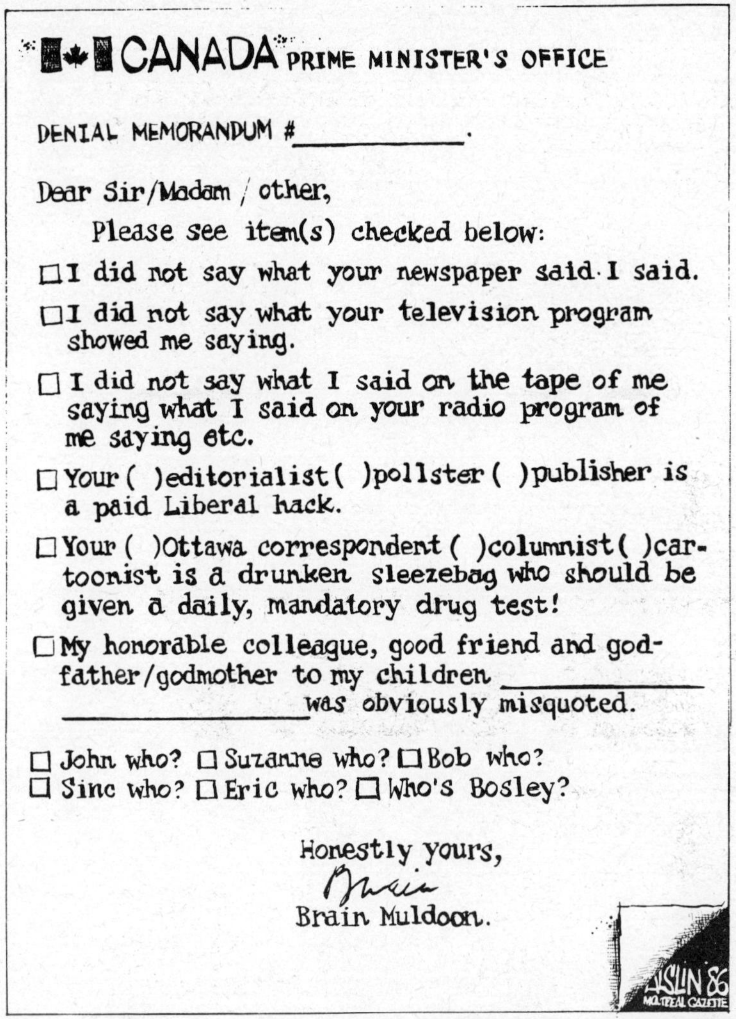
CANADA PRIME MINISTER'S OFFICE
DENIAL MEMORANDUM #___________.
Dear Sir/Madam / other,
Please see item(s) checked below:
☐ I did not say what your newspaper said I said.
☐ I did not say what your television program showed me saying.
☐ I did not say what I said on the tape of me saying what I said on your radio program of me saying etc.
☐ Your ( )editorialist ( )pollster ( )publisher is a paid Liberal hack.
☐ Your ( )Ottawa correspondent ( )columnist ( )cartoonist is a drunken sleezebag who should be given a daily, mandatory drug test!
☐ My honorable colleague, good friend and godfather/godmother to my children ___________ ___________ was obviously misquoted.
☐ John who? ☐ Suzanne who? ☐ Bob who?
☐ Sinc who? ☐ Eric who? ☐ Who's Bosley?
Honestly yours,
Brain Muldoon.
AISLIN '86 MONTREAL GAZETTE

- N.D.P. CONVENTION IN MONTREAL.

AISLIN '86
MONTREAL
GAZETTE

-RUMORS OF TRUDEAU RETURN.

· ANDRE OUELETTE CALLS COLLEAGUE DON JOHNSTON A WESTMOUNT RHODESIAN.

UNPUBLISHED.

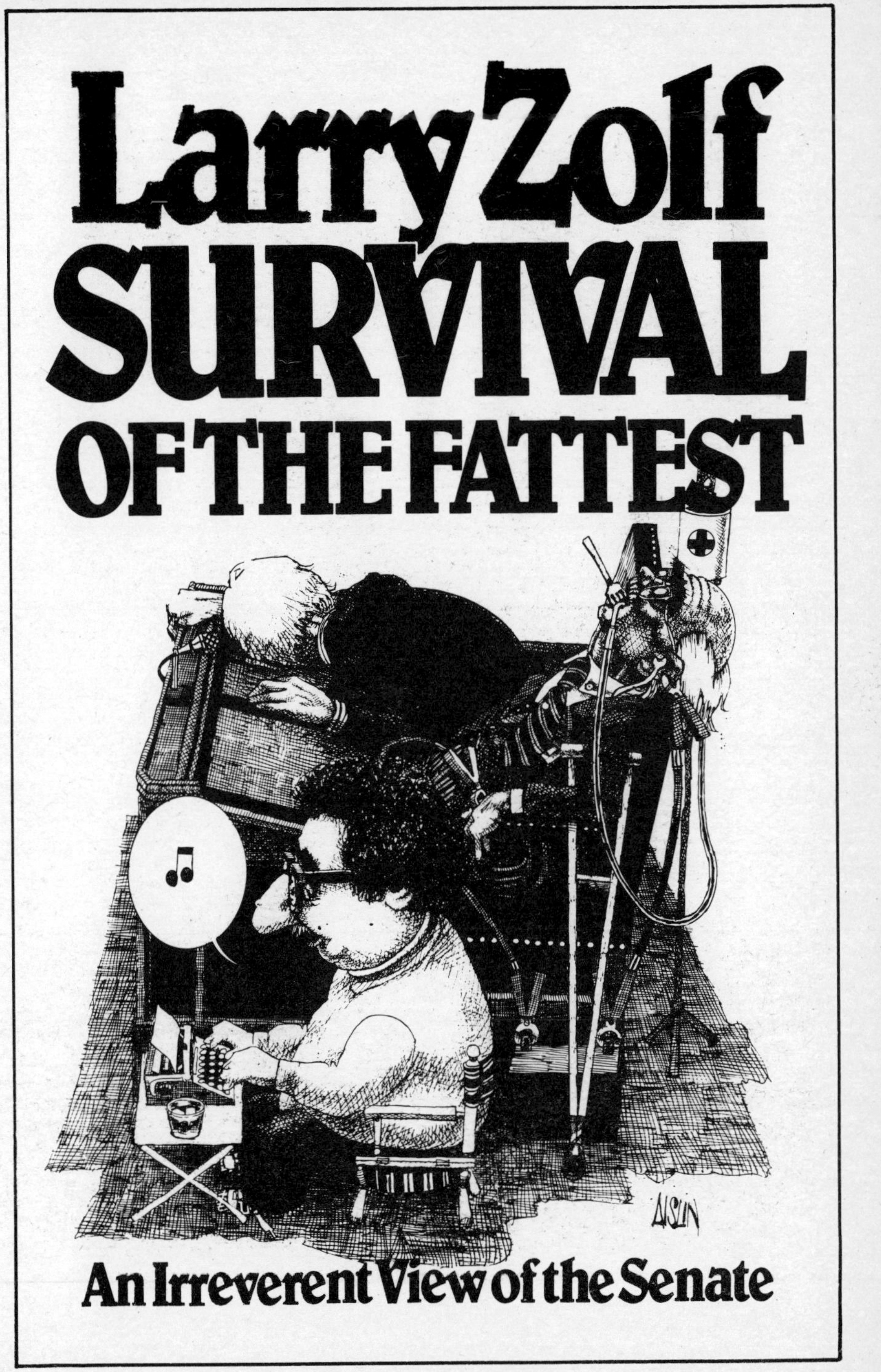

AISLIN'S BESTIARY
LESTER LIZARD
LAWYER. SENIOR PARTNER IN LIZARD, LIZARD, REPTILE AND LIZARD WHERE HE MOVES PIECES OF NOTARIZED PAPER AROUND HIS DESK FOR SIX FIGURES A YEAR...
AISLIN 86
TORONTO STAR

ANDY SADOWSKI
UNION ORGANIZER WHO BELIEVES IN EQUALITY FOR ALL; LOUSY DANCER; TERRIBLE TIPPER.
AISLIN 85
TORONTO STAR

LEON B. CUDA
NO ONE KNOWS ANYTHING ABOUT THE MYSTERIOUS GENTLEMAN IN APARTMENT 1409 WHO ALWAYS SMILES ON THE ELEVATOR, EVEN WHEN HE'S ALONE... IMPORT AND EXPORT.

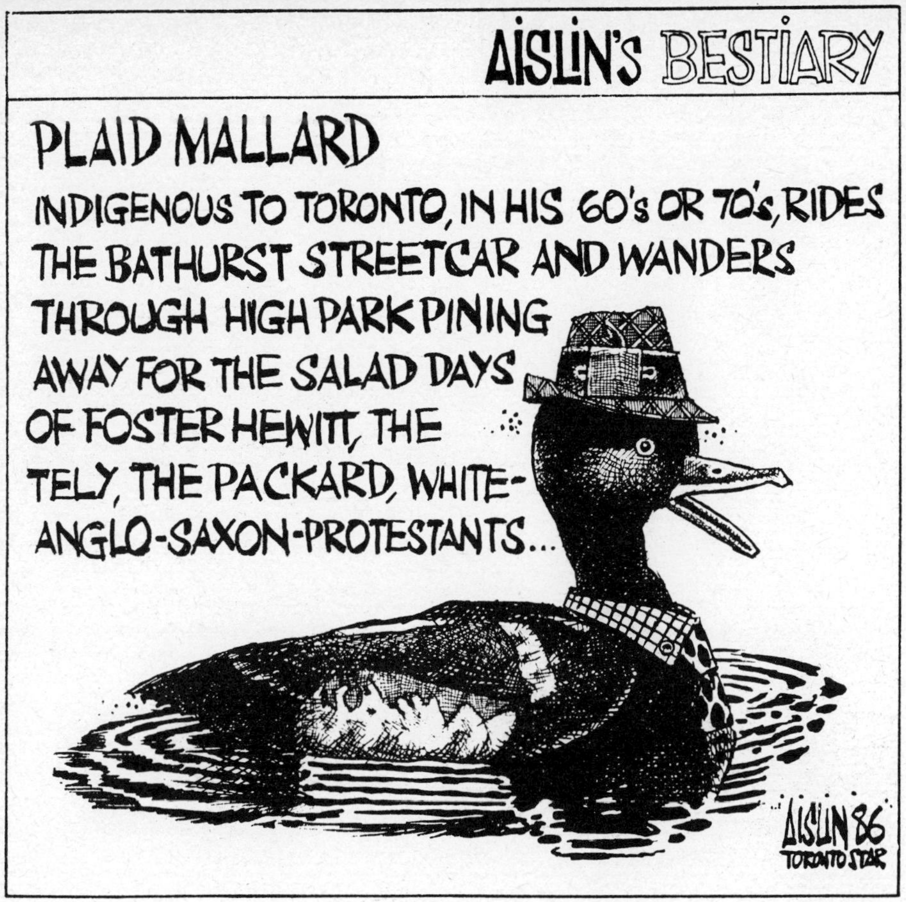
AISLIN'S BESTIARY
PLAID MALLARD
INDIGENOUS TO TORONTO, IN HIS 60's OR 70's, RIDES THE BATHURST STREETCAR AND WANDERS THROUGH HIGH PARK PINING AWAY FOR THE SALAD DAYS OF FOSTER HEWITT, THE TELY, THE PACKARD, WHITE-ANGLO-SAXON-PROTESTANTS...
AISLIN 86
TORONTO STAR

MUNGO DROSS
VOTED "MOST LIKELY TO SUCCEED" BY YOUNG FASCISTS OF ROYAL YORK COLLEGIATE INSTITUTE, MUNGO PARLAYED HIS KNOWLEDGE OF FOUR CHORDS INTO GRUNGY ORFICE, THE WORLD'S LOUDEST HEAVY METAL BAND. PRESENTLY SEEKING TAX ADVICE, HAVEN AND/OR LOOPHOLES...
AISLIN 85
TORONTO STAR

DEIRDRE SIDESADDLE
CLOTHES by DALLAS; BRAIN by PEOPLE MAGAZINE; VOCABULARY by ENTERTAINMENT TONIGHT; KARMA by U.S.A. TODAY.
AISLIN 85
TORONTO STAR

AISLIN'S BESTIARY
HERB SPINDLE
OFFICE COMPTROLLER, GOSSIP AND COWARD; IN CHARGE OF MOVING PAPER FROM POINT 'J' TO POINT 'W'; ALWAYS FIRST WITH THE LATEST SEXIST/RACIST JOKE, HIS DREAMS ARE DOMINATED BY MONSTER EROTIC FISHING LURES AND FLIES.
AISLIN 85
TORONTO STAR

LEO ROCKBOTTOM
CANADIAN FOOTBALLER WHO IS OVERWORKED AND UNDERPAID WHEN COMPARED TO HIS BASEBALL AND HOCKEY COUSINS; CAN'T ENJOY THE FINER THINGS IN LIFE; DRIVES A LADA; GETS OFF ON 222's AND COUGH SYRUP.
AISLIN 85
TORONTO STAR

GEORGE R. BELFRY the 3d.
BLIND; HAS 15% HEARING IN ONE EAR; SPEAKS WITH A LISP; WORST DRESSED MAN OF THE PAST DECADE; LAST SEXUAL DALLIANCE IN 1948; EDITORIAL PAGE WRITER... LIBERAL.

MILLICENT ORANGE

MILLICENT KNOWS WHO IS RESPONSIBLE FOR SUCH THINGS AS FLOPPY DISCS, METRICS, POSTAL CODES, FIBRE OPTICS, SUSHI, TOFUTTI, TELECONFERENCING, AEROBICS, VHS, BETA, VCR AND ANYTHING DIGITAL! THOSE FOREIGN FRENCH, THAT'S WHO... AND SHE WANTS TO KNOW WHAT HER BRIAN MULRONEY IS GOING TO DO ABOUT IT.

AISLIN'S BESTIARY

DEIRDRE GLEBE

PROFESSIONAL STUDENT. AFTER 14 YEARS OF STUDY, SHE RECENTLY RECEIVED HER P.H.D. ON THE SUBJECT OF HITTITE INFLUENCES ON EARLY OSHAWA FOLK SONGS, AT A MERE COLLECTIVE COST OF $310,000 TO THE TAXPAYER. LIVING PROOF OF THE ANCIENT HAIDA MAXIM, "PEOPLE WHO WEAR SENSIBLE SHOES ALWAYS HAVE TERRIBLE SEX."

SID CARP

MARGARINE AND GUN SALESMAN; DRINKS HIS RYE OUT OF A STEIN; ATTIRE BY MISTER MUFFLER; NO NONSENSE KIND OF A GUY, HE THINKS AIDS IS THE GREATEST THING SINCE COMBAT BOOTS.

SPORTS...

• MONTREAL ALOUETTES FOLD.

DRUGS-A MAJOR INFLUENCE IN HOCKEY? I SAY, "NONSENSE!!"
NOW, THIS, FROM OUR SPONSOR...
GLUG-GLUGLUG-GLUG
AISLIN 86
MTL. GAZETTE.

...AND THE LARGE BUILDING RIGHT BESIDE THE STADIUM IS A DRUG REHABILITATION CENTRE.
STADIUM
AISLIN 86
MONTREAL GAZETTE

GREY CUPS
AISLIN 85
MONTREAL GAZETTE

"BUT, DOUG, IT'S 6:15 am... THE GAME DOESN'T START FOR 14 HOURS."...

- RED SOX VERSUS METS.

AISLIN '86
MONTREAL GAZETTE
C'MON, HARRY, YOU PROMISED ME JUNE...
YOU SAID THAT HOCKEY WOULD BE OVER...
THAT FOOTBALL WOULDN'T HAVE STARTED...
AND THAT YOU'D ONLY GET INTERESTED IN BASEBALL AFTER THE JULY ALL-STAR BREAK!
HARRY?
CLICK...
AND NOW, FROM MEXICO...
WORLD CUP SOCCER

-DON CHERRY.

BUT WHY BRING IT BACK IF IT WON'T DO ANY GOOD?
BECAUSE, MY SHRINK TELLS ME, A MAJORITY OF US CANADIANS HAVE A MORBID OBSESSION TO WITNESS THE DOMINATION OF THOSE WE HATE AND FEAR THROUGH VENGEFUL VIOLENCE LEADING TO PAIN, INJURY AND, HOPEFULLY, DEATH ...AND WE'RE JUST NOT GETTING EN-OUGH ANYMORE TO SATISFY OUR CRAVINGS FROM HOCKEY.
AISLIN 87
MONTREAL GAZETTE

THE TORIES-PART THREE...
AISLIN 86.
MONTREAL GAZETTE.

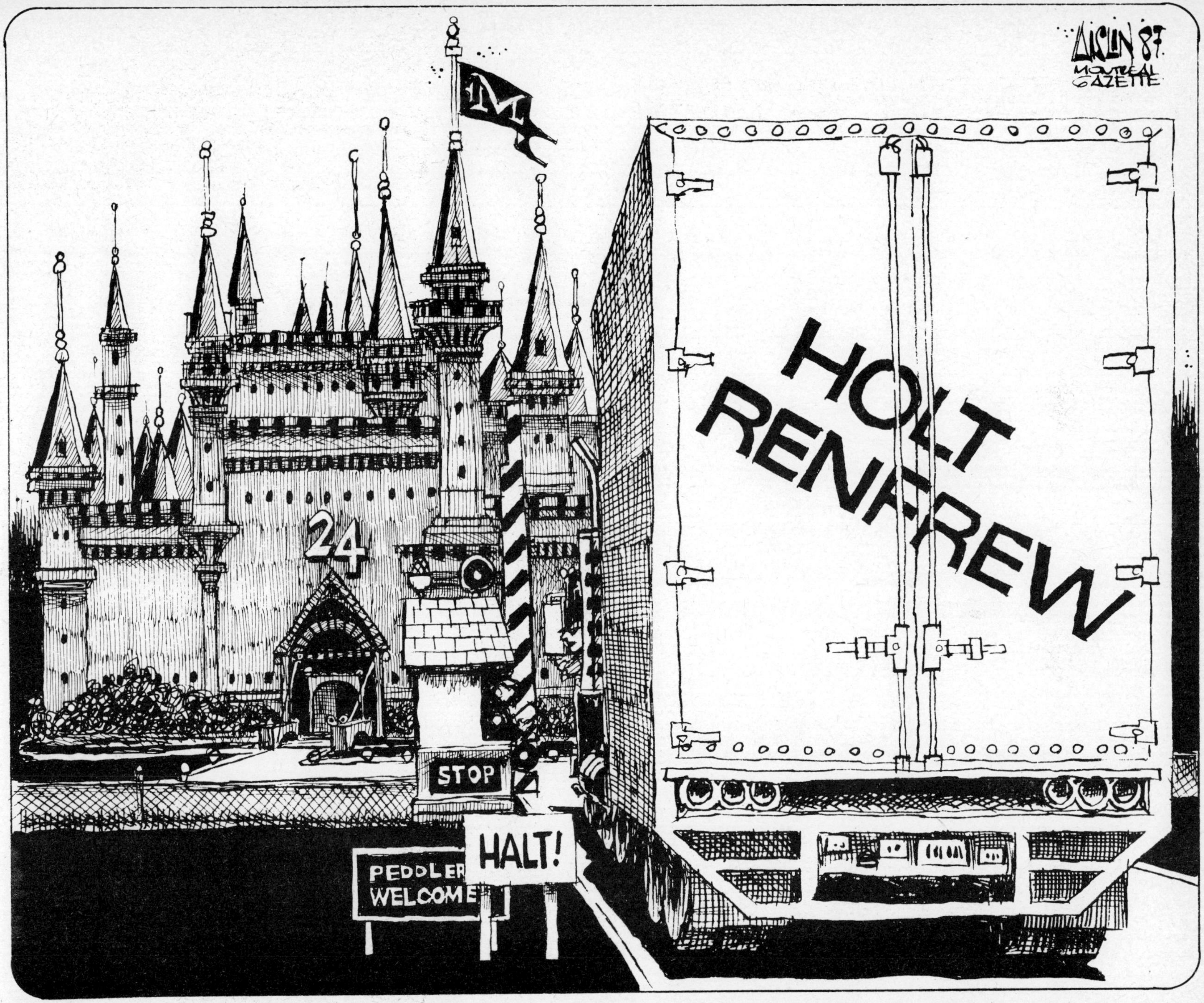

"I'VE GOT ANOTHER LOAD OF SHOES AND CLOTHES FOR IMELDA MULDOON."

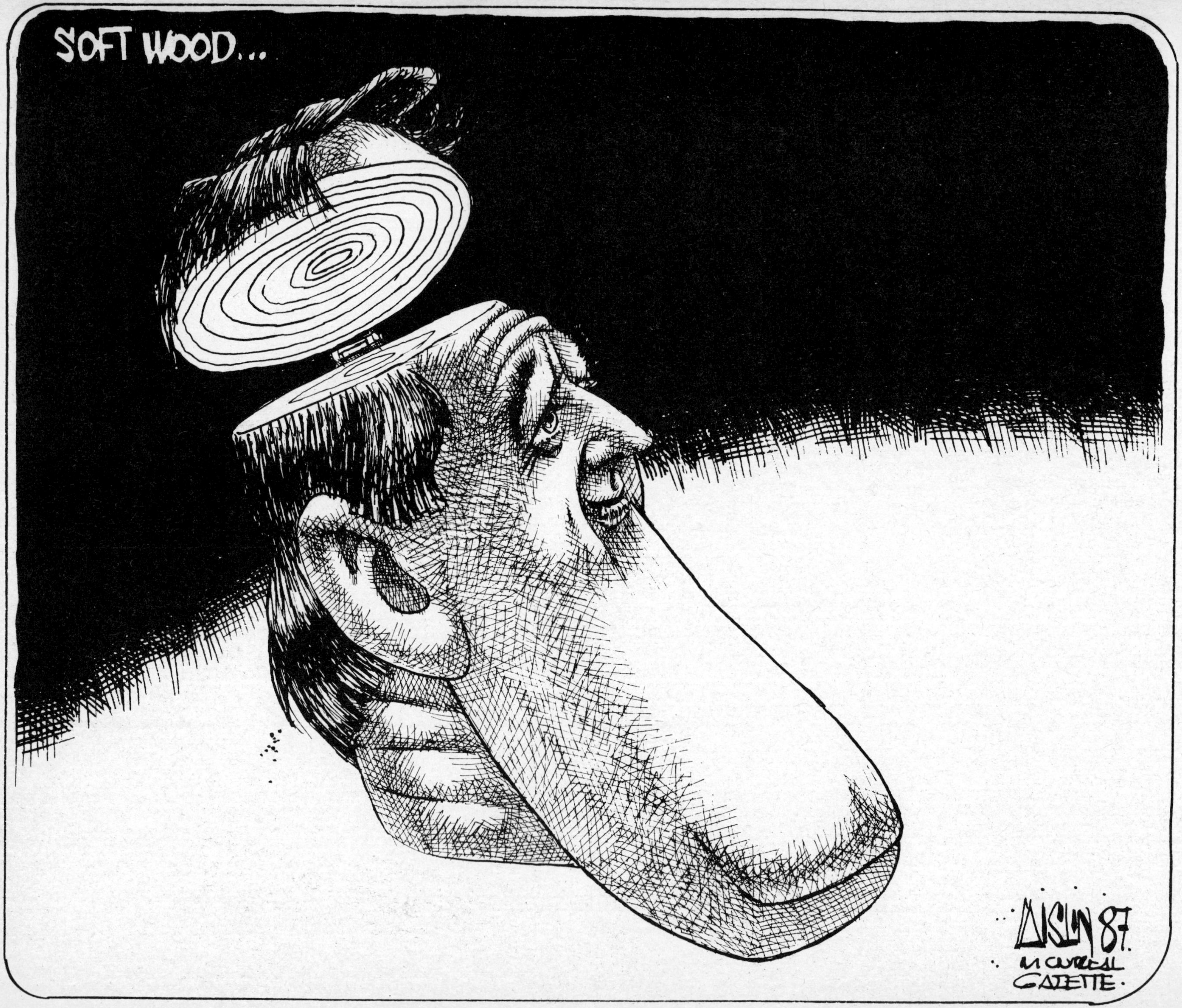
SOFT WOOD...
AISLIN 87.
MONTREAL GAZETTE.

AISLIN 86 MONTREAL GAZETTE
HEH, HEH... SAY, THAT REMINDS ME...
GEEZ, HE'S OPENING HIS MOUTH IN PUBLIC AGAIN!! PHONE DALTON FAST.

...PACKAGE FOR YOUR PRESS SECRETARY.
PMO
RECEPTION
SALT PETRE

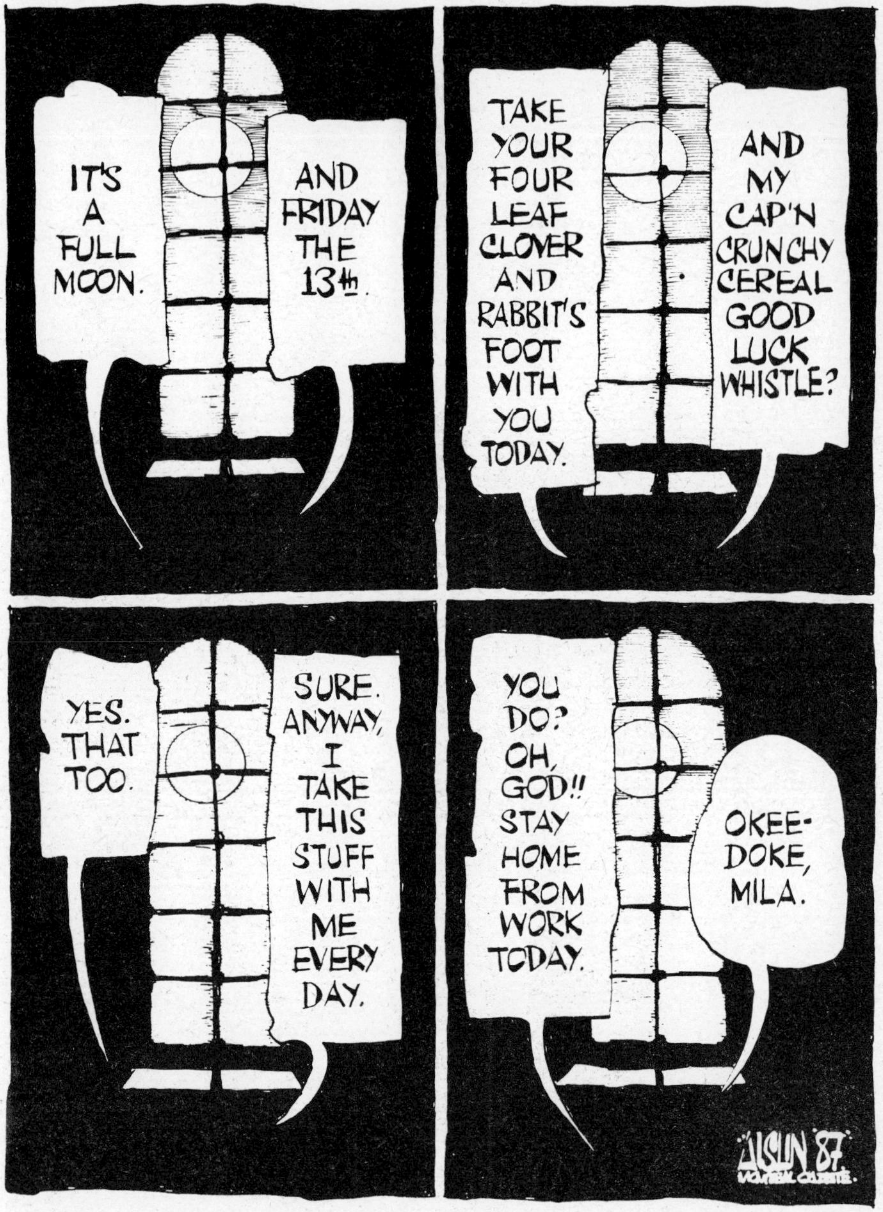
IT'S A FULL MOON.
AND FRIDAY THE 13th.
TAKE YOUR FOUR LEAF CLOVER AND RABBIT'S FOOT WITH YOU TODAY.
AND MY CAP'N CRUNCHY CEREAL GOOD LUCK WHISTLE?
YES. THAT TOO.
SURE. ANYWAY, I TAKE THIS STUFF WITH ME EVERY DAY.
YOU DO? OH, GOD!! STAY HOME FROM WORK TODAY.
OKEE-DOKE, MILA.
AISLIN '87

POLL: LESS THAN ONE CANADIAN IN FOUR SUPPORTS THE TORIES.

• P.M. TOURS AFRICA.

FINALLY!! A COW TO MILK.
AND HE WILL, HE WILL...
CONSTITUTION
GUCCI DAIRY
AISLIN 87.
MONTREAL GAZETTE.

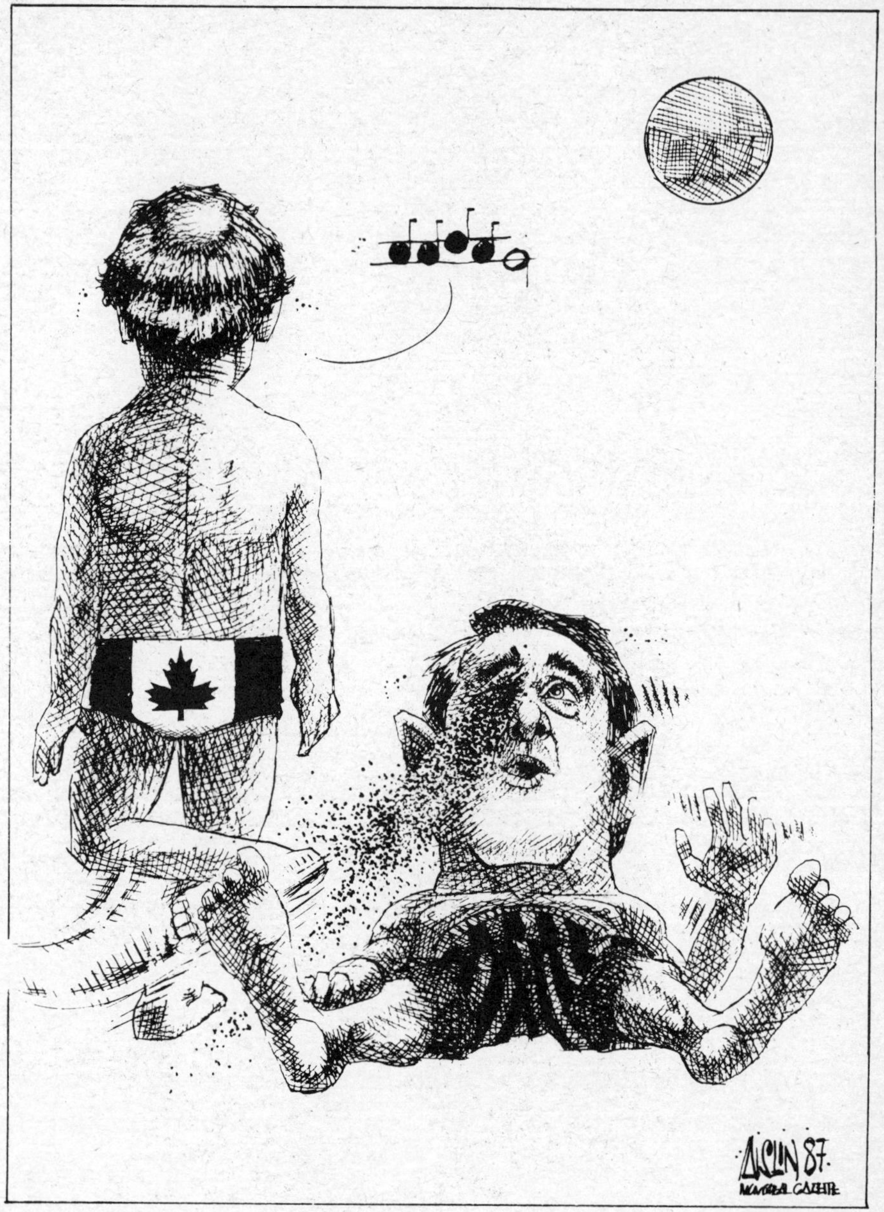

• TRUDEAU COMMENTS ON MEECH LAKE.

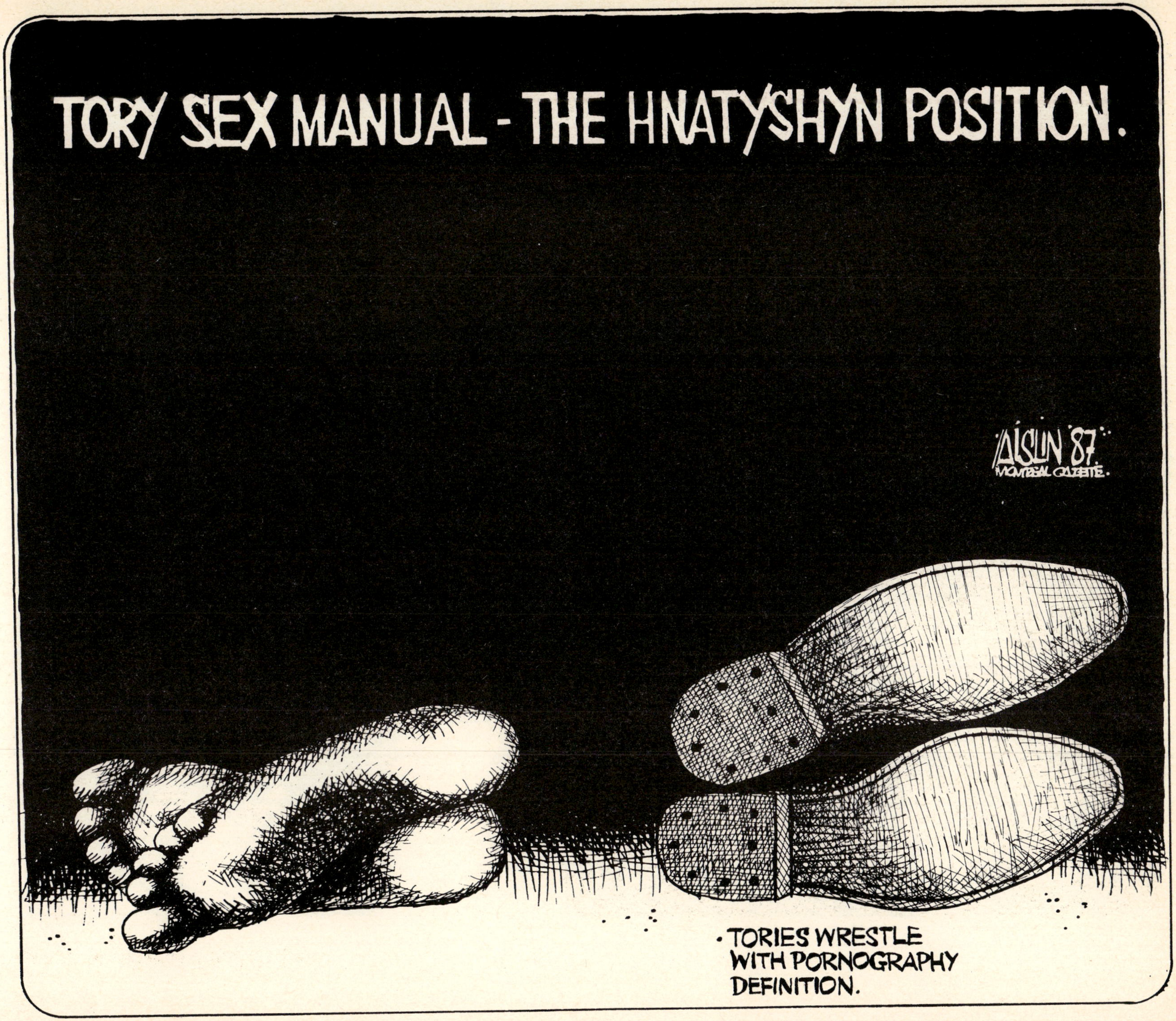
TORY SEX MANUAL - THE HNATYSHYN POSITION.
AISLIN '87
MONTREAL GAZETTE.
• TORIES WRESTLE
WITH PORNOGRAPHY
DEFINITION.

·VENICE SUMMIT.

· TO BE CONTINUED...